UNTETHERED
The True Children of Cyrus

Brian Alikhani and Rosalyn R. Hafner

Copyright © 2016 Brian Alikhani & Rosalyn R. Hafner
All rights reserved.

ISBN: 154125144X
ISBN 13: 9781541251441

One day I'm gonna fly away
One day when heaven calls my name
I lay down; I close my eyes at night
I can see morning in light …
—Arash, "One Day"

CONTENTS

Preface   vii

Chapter 1   Anticipation and Anxiety   1
Chapter 2   Arriving in America   9
Chapter 3   Lake Tahoe   15
Chapter 4   A New Year   19
Chapter 5   Grades   26
Chapter 6   There She Is   34
Chapter 7   Lake Tahoe Again   43
Chapter 8   Close Encounters   53
Chapter 9   Unexpected News   64
Chapter 10 Feeling Satiated   71
Chapter 11 New Friends   75
Chapter 12 Persian Friends   96
Chapter 13 Driving   105
Chapter 14 Starting School   122
Chapter 15 Girls   134
Chapter 16 The Celebration of the Persian Empire   138
Chapter 17 Sara   141
Chapter 18 The Ayatollah   154
Chapter 19 Breaking Up   167
Chapter 20 As Adults   170

Chapter 21	The Last Days of the Shah	176
Chapter 22	The Hostage Crisis and the Iranian Revolution	178
Chapter 23	Ten Factors	186
Chapter 24	Children of Cyrus	189

PREFACE

I have been holding my story inside for too long—not the story of me as an immigrant per se but the story of me as an involuntary immigrant, a young student who could not return to my country of origin because of the events taking place there while I attended school halfway around the world.

When I was sixteen years old, I left a vibrant, modern Tehran to attend high school in San Jose, California. Within the first few months, as I was adjusting to classes taught in a foreign language, my sisters and I watched on TV how protestors became revolutionaries, how the shah became a despised leader both to his citizens and to the world, and how so much attention was given to a relatively unknown, exiled religious man. In disbelief, my friends, family, and I stood on the sidelines and witnessed Khomeini, a cleric who disdained modernization, destroy the very fabric of our country and fling Iran back into the dark ages by orchestrating the ouster of the shah and taking over as the new supreme leader.

It is important that I tell this story not as a recounting of historical events but of how the historical events affected me, my people, and the world and of how the news reports at the time influenced the outcome.

In telling my story, I collaborated with Rosalyn R. Hafner, a friend and colleague who, like a painter, took the sketch of the story and added the color, making the details come to life.

Brian Alikhani

CHAPTER 1
ANTICIPATION AND ANXIETY

Anticipation and anxiety competed in short spurts to be my leading emotion as I prepared to leave my homeland, Iran, and fly halfway around the world to attend an American high school. I was leaving a calm, stable country to go to the other side of the world. I became a walking invitation for my classmates and family to share warnings, rumors, and admonitions about America. "Don't go out after dark. Everyone owns a gun." "My cousin went there, and someone stole his wallet. It had his passport in it, and now he's stuck." "Whatever you do, don't get mixed up with the communists or the disco clubbers." That last warning came from my father. No one foresaw the dark clouds of the political storm that was brewing on the horizon of time and that would alter the course of my country for generations to come.

A week before my departure, my mother bought me a large, expandable black suitcase. To get it, she had to go to the southern part of Tehran to shop at the bazaar, or free market. Most of the vendors were shrewd religious businessmen, and they would turn out to be one of the main sources of unrest against the shah. My sister Anahita, who had also been accepted to the American high school, received the exact same suitcase. That was the only exact same thing about us besides the fact that we were twins. My last week in Tehran, the black suitcase squatted on my bedroom floor like an uninvited guest, reminding me every day that I would soon be somewhere completely foreign. What kept me going was knowing that I would return to the comfort and familiarity of my home and my family and be able to get a good job. I planned on studying hard so that eventually I could move up the ranks to become an executive or a government official. Those with education had lots of opportunity to be successful. Knowing that I would be able to come back and be successful gave me a sense of encouragement to deal with the unknown.

A couple of days before our departure, my older brother, Farhad, called my sister and me to the dining room and unfolded a map of the United States of America. Farhad assumed an air of authority, not only because he was six and a half years older than my sister and me but also because of his innate sense of confidence, which came partly from his Al Pacino looks. His jet-black hair, light skin, and dark eyes attracted many girls, which made me jealous at times. Even though he was married at nineteen, girls got giddy in his presence. He was familiar with Europe and the United States, having been to both places many times to study English and do work for his business.

He placed the map on top of a large piece of paper that covered the wooden dining table. He then scooted the map to the left and began to draw on the paper that extended past the right edge of the map. I immediately recognized Europe and Africa, even before he labeled them. With more detail, he outlined Iran and labeled the bordering countries to the west, Turkey and Iraq. Iran looked millions of miles from America. There was so much land and ocean to cross. Anxiety was overcoming anticipation as I studied my brother's map.

"Borz and Anahita, I want to show you where we will fly and what stops we will make," Farhad said as he drew a line with his pencil from Tehran to Germany. "Even though I will be escorting you, I want you to know where you are going. It is a very long way, and we will need to stop a couple of times before we get to San Francisco. Look: here is Frankfurt, Germany. This will be our first stop. We have an eight-hour layover there. When we get off the plane, we first must figure out what gate our next plane will leave from. We are going to change airlines and fly on PanAm from Germany to the United States. Our first stop in the United States will be New York City, which is about here." Farhad stabbed the large dot labeled New York City with his pen. "When we are in New York City, we will have to go through customs and immigration. That means we will have to show our passports and visas, and they may look in our suitcases. We only have two and a half hours in New York City, which isn't much time, so we are going to have to be diligent in trying to get through the lines as quickly as possible. Don't be rude to people, but don't hang back. Once we are through customs and immigration, we will need to immediately find our gate for the plane that will take us to San Francisco. Look here: it is on the other side of the country. The United States is much larger than Iran. See this state up here? That is Alaska, and it belongs to the United States. Alaska is a little larger than Iran, so you can see how big the whole country of the United States is."

Anahita and I already knew the geography of the United States and the world well enough, so I looked at Farhad a bit strangely, wondering why he felt he had to explain the map to us.

"I suggest you sleep as much as you can on the planes so that when we get to the airports, you will have the energy to move quickly to find our gates," my brother went on. "It's going to take us at least thirty hours to get to San Francisco from here. Once we are there, our sister Jasmin will meet us and drive us to San Jose.

"It's going to be a very long journey. I don't want you ever to lose sight of each other. Airports in foreign countries are extremely large and full of people, and I don't want either of you to get lost. Look out for each other," he admonished as he started to fold up the map. "If you do get lost, find a police officer or security guard."

I looked at Anahita. She was equally puzzled by Farhad's geography lecture. Other than Anahita's and my light-brown hair, people could not tell that we were related, let alone that we were twins. But I knew Anahita as only a twin can. Her full lips had turned slightly down to express impatience while at the same time her deep brown eyes had narrowed behind her studious-looking glasses. That meant that she too was a little anxious to be making the journey. Anahita was the quiet person in the family. She would often look up sadly from her book of poetry or novel of unrequited love when we asked her something and interrupted her reading. She would disappear for hours at a time, bent over a book or curled up on the couch, lost in the fantasies of fiction. Sometimes you had to nudge her just to make her say something.

"I'll make sure Borz stays with me. He's the one that almost didn't even get to go," Anahita said with an air of superiority in her voice. I winced inside, remembering the ordeal I'd had to go through to get my F1 visa. For some unknown reason, even though we'd applied at the same time and my father had scrupulously examined both of our applications to make sure there were no mistakes before submitting them, the US embassy had granted my sister her F1 visa and rejected my application. I had to obtain the I-20 form, or a "Certificate of Eligibility for Nonimmigrant Students." The US embassy questioned why I was applying to go to a public high school, which meant that American taxpayers would pay for my education (though they had no qualms about my sister's application to attend the same high school). My father said that different people must have processed the two applications. "Nothing is black and white, my children. It all has to do with people and relationships. That is how government works," he explained, slowly shaking his head.

A few days after I received the rejection notice, my father took me back to the US embassy. He dressed in one of his expensive suits and put on his favorite aftershave, which I always thought gave off the scent of a sophisticated man. We met with a consular officer I hadn't seen in my previous visit, a middle-aged Japanese American woman. When she looked up from her desk and saw my dad, with his Tony Curtis looks and dark, curly hair, she smiled and gave him her full attention. She listened patiently to my father as he explained why we were there. He said that he had sent his older two children to the United States to have the opportunity to get a superior education, one that could not be attained in Iran. My father himself had gone to culinary school in France and was now successful in the restaurant business in Tehran. He went on to explain that he wanted the best for his children and that it was important they be well educated so they could return to Iran and make a good living. He said that it was his youngest children's turn to go to the United States and that our older sister was already there waiting for us. He explained that his oldest son, Farhad, had returned from the United States in 1977 and managed his own little clothing boutique in Tehran. He told her how Farhad traveled to France and the UK frequently to purchase merchandise for his store.

After laying my application on her desk, the American consulate smiled, reached into her desk drawer, pulled out a small bottle of Wite-Out, and began painting over the parts of the form that she felt we had answered incorrectly. Being fifteen, I had used Wite-Out many times in school but was surprised it would pass on an official document. My father and I looked at each other as she carefully painted between the lines. His eyebrows were lifted, but his eyes silently commanded me not to say a word. Two weeks before my scheduled departure, my visa came.

We lived in the affluent part of Tehran, located in the north. Like most other homes in Tehran, our home was built of cement. There were two separate units. My dad supplemented his income by renting the other unit to a civil engineer and his wife and young son. I liked the man because he always smiled and said hello when he entered the compound and saw me. Our home was dark gray on the outside with gates in front. It was large enough for our family but was not considered a mansion. Most of our neighbors were Americans who worked in the automobile, computer manufacturing, petroleum, and airline industries, among others. They were always friendly to us and often asked for recommendations of great places to eat. I would usually spot Farhad chatting with our American friends when I returned home from school.

The night before we were to depart, my parents invited all our relatives and a few friends over for a farewell party. A feast of juicy lamb kebabs; fresh celery stew; dark, aromatic eggplant stew; and various soups, or *aush*, colorfully covered the dining room table. Mom made sure there were plenty of lamb kebabs for Anahita and *loubia polo*, my favorite rice and fresh green beans dish, for me. I ate like there was no tomorrow, or at least like there was not going to be any more meals like this in the near future.

Everyone chatted excitedly as if at a celebration, not a farewell-for-a-long-time gathering. Popular songs played scratchily on the record player. It was a typical party, similar to ones I had been to many times before for birthdays, weddings, and the births of cousins. No one asked me how I felt about going abroad or where exactly I was going or if I planned on keeping in touch. Everyone seemed more interested in gossiping or talking about politics.

Before I went to bed, I opened my packed suitcase and checked all the contents one more time. At the last minute, I threw in my prized kite. When I had packed my suitcase that morning, I'd decided that I was too old to take the kite with me, but with my flight only a few hours away, I felt better packing it.

At the beginning of summer break, I had built the kite out of plastic. In Iran, kids of my age flew handmade kites from age eight up to eighteen. Sometimes even guys in their twenties would fly kites, probably because they were reluctant to give up a childhood pastime that gave them so much pleasure. Unlike in neighboring countries where kites were flown like aerial dogfights, in Iran the purpose was to make the prettiest kite that flew the longest.

All my friends' kites were constructed from paper and wood, but my kite was special. It wasn't the fastest kite on the block, but since I'd painted it with my favorite colors, red and blue, it looked a lot like the Union Jack and was very noticeable as it zigzagged above the rooftops. When people saw it tugging at its string as if trying to escape, they thought it was a sign that the British were going to invade Iran again. Neighbors were shocked and relieved when they saw that it was just me on the other end of the string.

When all our friends had gone back to school in September, Anahita and I had stayed home, waiting for our visas to come. Anahita had fallen into the rabbit hole of reading and had finished dozens of novels and poems. Reading was Anahita's thing, not mine. I'd spent hours honing the technique of kite flying and had become like a skilled puppeteer deftly controlling his marionette. My kite had taken on a personality, as it had the freedom to look down on everything. I would pretend it was a spy, and when it got too close to the rooftops, I would yank it up with a swift snap of my wrist.

When Mom woke me the morning I was to leave, it felt as if I had just fallen asleep. My eyes stung, and I felt light-headed sitting up. I carefully dressed in the new shirt and trousers that Mom had laid out for me, aware that the next time I dressed, she would not be there to lay out my clothes.

"You look like you haven't slept at all, Borz," Farhad said as he lugged Anahita's suitcase outside. "It's a big day. We're going to America! I'm so excited to go back. I wish you looked more excited."

Farhad, who was married and seven years older than me, had already spent three years in the United States. He had studied American literature at Oklahoma State University and returned to Tehran in the summer of 1977. With his superior English skills, confident manner, and international experience, Farhad was the next best thing to having my father with me.

"Is your suitcase ready? I'll take it out to the car. Anahita's is so heavy that the plane might not be able to fly with it!"

My parents drove Farhad, Anahita, and me to the airport. A procession of twenty relatives crammed into a few small cars followed us. Unlike the party the night before, everyone seemed subdued. I had a strange sense that this was going to be a longer journey for me than planned. I felt a sense of unrest, yet, around me, my family was calm. Iran was calm.

CHAPTER 2
ARRIVING IN AMERICA

An hour from JFK, I dozed off in my window seat. The cold glass cooled my forehead. My cramped body felt as if it had been sitting in a chair for a week, not just the eleven hours from Frankfurt. When the stewardess announced that we would be landing soon in New York City, I stretched my legs under the seat in front of me and gazed out the porthole window of the plane. During our circumnavigation of the globe, the date had advanced to December 11, 1977. Coming in for a landing was exciting, and I gazed out at the lights of New York City, which dazzled like a crown's jewels in the nighttime sky. As we came in closer, I could see that the large black swaths between the masses of sparkling lights were bodies of water. I put my shoes on and prepared to walk off the plane and into America.

It was late at night, yet the airport was crowded with passengers and greeters. There was no order to anything or anyone, or so it seemed. Farhad led the way, navigating us expertly through the crowds. It was all I could do to keep up with him as I dodged pushy people, noisy kids, and large suitcases. He led us to an underground train that took us to another section of the massive airport. The room for immigration inspection was larger than my gymnasium at school. Officers funneled everyone into different lines, which were all endlessly long. I had lost track of what time or day it was and felt disoriented and drained yet excited and eager to get to our destination. As we approached the immigration officer, Farhad told us to take out our passports and visas. The immigration officer asked Farhad many questions, way more than he had asked the people ahead of us. Anahita and I let Farhad do the talking because neither one of us could speak English well. The US immigration officer finally stamped my Iranian passport with an F1 visa entry that showed JFK as the port of entry. I had made it.

The next task was to find our luggage and go through customs. It was confusing to me that we had to get our luggage and then resubmit it when in Frankfurt the luggage had gone on the flight to New York City without us having to do anything. When we found the American Airlines gate for our flight to San Francisco, we all collapsed into seats in the waiting area, relieved and exhausted.

Once on the plane, with our seat belts on, I slept until the stewardess announced that we were preparing to land. Thanks to the sleeping, the flight time went by in a blink.

Our seventeen-year-old sister, Jasmin, stood at the gate craning her neck to see over the crowd disembarking the flight. I saw Jasmin before she saw me, and I waved. Spotting me, she started jumping up and down, her light-brown hair bouncing and her hazel eyes shining. Her warm smile immediately made me feel less like I had just arrived in a foreign country. She wrapped my sister and me in her familiar embrace and fired questions at us, asking about our trip. Jasmin was energetic and talkative, unlike Anahita, who tended to drift away during discussions. Farhad, who was last to reach her, gave her a hug and proclaimed that Anahita and I had been good travelers and that we had never complained the whole way. Traveling without my parents was very grown up, and I puffed up with pride for being acknowledged for traveling halfway around the world without complaining.

After Anahita and I found our matching black suitcases on the baggage carousel and Farhad grabbed his smaller suitcase, we followed Jasmin through throngs of people to the parking garage. Outside, the morning sunshine and clear air greeted me with a warm, welcoming embrace. I had stepped out of the gray concrete world of Tehran and into the slightly cloudy but bright and colorful world of San Francisco. The ocean breeze, like laughter, lightened the grogginess I felt from traveling for forty-eight hours.

We piled the suitcases into the trunk of Jasmin's new 1977 orange Toyota Corolla, which my father had bought for her on a visit six months ago. Jasmin had lived with Farhad and his wife, Salma, in Oklahoma while she'd finished her last years in high school there. When Farhad and Salma had returned to Iran, Jasmin had moved to San Jose to attend a community college. Salma's brother and cousins all lived in San Jose, and they had helped Jasmin get settled with an apartment and had showed her around.

Jasmin got behind the wheel, and Farhad sat next to her. Anahita and I climbed into the backseat. "Don't put your shoes on the seat, Borz. This is a new car. Put your seat belts on, everyone. It's the law here, and I don't want to get pulled over," Jasmin ordered.

Even though Jasmin had only been driving for a short while, she expertly handled the traffic and freeways. I had never been on a road where cars went so fast, and I found it unnerving that no cars ran into each as they passed within inches of others. I surveyed the scenery that flew by, trying to take it in as my new home. California looked colorful in contrast to where I had come from. From that point on, Iran would always be gray in my mind's eye.

"Hey, Borz and Anahita," Farhad said, turning around to face us, "we are on Highway 101 now. It goes all the way from the Canadian border in the north to the Mexican border in the south. It is over fifteen hundred miles long. Isn't that amazing? That's farther than going from Tehran way down to Bandar Abbas in the far south."

I realized that we were one small blip on a road that stretched hundreds of miles and wondered how people could possibly have built it. If I could see from above, like my kite could, our car would be a small orange particle in a long line of particles.

"Borz! We are talking to you," Jasmin yelled, breaking my train of thought. "I'm trying to figure out what restaurant to go to. What do you want to eat? Not everything is open because it's Sunday."

"I don't care," I replied, just wanting to get back to thinking about the longest road I had ever been on.

Jasmin parked outside a restaurant with a large yellow-and-red sign that said Denny's. A lady showed us to a booth and handed us oversize plastic menus. The chatter of people speaking English at nearby tables emphasized my uneasiness of feeling foreign. Having studied English for six months in Iran with a teacher who struggled with the language himself didn't help much. I could read the menu but had difficulty understanding the waitress and her laid-back manner of speaking. Jasmin suggested that I order a plain omelet. Omelets now always remind me of my first American meal, the first food I ate on the other side of the world from my home.

Our tea came first. Like all Persians, we only drank coffee on special occasions. Tea was our everyday beverage. Later in my life I discovered that Persians used to indulge in coffee on a daily basis three hundred years ago. They switched to tea during the reign of King Nader Shah, who was cultivating relationships with Persia's northern neighbor, Russia. My family back home had a samovar for heating the water for tea. I always thought that the samovar was a Persian invention and was shocked when I learned that they came from Russia.

The waitress brought our food in one trip, balancing the plates along her arm. She named each plate as she set it down in front of us. After we had all taken a few bites, she returned to our table and asked if there was anything else she could get us. Americans seemed very friendly; at least this waitress did.

We all felt overfull as we left the restaurant. It was midmorning, and the fog had cleared, exposing a bright blue sky that made the sun's reflection off cars blinding as we drove to Jasmin's apartment in south San Jose. She lived in a large complex that was beautifully landscaped. The grounds looked lush with multiple shades of green displayed on the immense variety of plants.

When we entered Jasmin's apartment, Anahita and I were a little surprised to find out that there was only one bedroom. We looked at each other, wondering how we would all fit.

"Where are we all going to sleep, Jasmin?" Farhad asked. "You knew we were coming. Why didn't you rent a bigger place?"

"I tried, but there weren't any available in this building," Jasmin said. "Besides, I'm on the waiting list for a two-bedroom apartment that might come up next month, and then we can move into that. We'll just have to make do until a two bedroom becomes available." Jasmin explained to us that it wasn't easy to find apartment managers who would rent to a seventeen-year-old with a cosigner. Salma's brother, Ehsan, who was older and had great credit, was her cosigner. We were limited to that building, but it was at least pretty and modern.

We decided that the sisters would share the bedroom, and Farhad and I would sleep in the living room. After Jasmin showed us the large swimming pool, Jacuzzi, and recreation room with billiards and ping-pong, we agreed that we could handle the cramped quarters and wait for a two-bedroom apartment.

About a week after we arrived, Ehsan and his wife, Mahshid, invited us over for dinner. We drove to their apartment in Santa Clara. When Ehsan opened the door to let us in, the delicious smell of the Persian stew Mahshid was preparing greeted us, followed shortly by Ehsan's warm greetings. I noticed his lisp right away, which, along with his tall, thin frame, softened his masculine demeanor.

The savory smell of the familiar spices made me feel welcome before I even entered their apartment, transporting me back to my homeland. Mahshid came out of the kitchen drying her hands on a dish towel. She gave Anahita and me quick hugs and asked if we were hungry. "I'm always hungry for Persian stew," I said.

"He's always hungry for anything," Anahita chimed in, and everyone laughed.

I had seen Mahshid at her wedding to Ehsan in Tehran. She was probably eighteen years old at the time. Even though that was a few years ago, she still struck me as quite beautiful, with her light-brown eyes and light skin. Mahshid was quiet like Anahita but friendly and hospitable.

Ehsan was twenty-one years old and had come to the United States three years ago with Mahshid, who was also his first cousin. They had come to the United States to attend San Jose State. Ehsan was in his second year of a civil engineering degree. Mahshid was majoring in computer science. Marrying first or second cousins is encouraged in Iran. It is thought to be safer to marry someone as familiar as a cousin than a complete stranger. The custom did not seem odd to me, as it was predetermined that I was going to marry my first cousin Narges. Unknown to us at the time, our destinies changed when I boarded the plane to come to the United States.

Ehsan helped Anahita and me with all our paperwork before we came to the United States as well as after we arrived. He gave Jasmin the list of school supplies that Andrew Hill High School had sent over, along with a stack of papers for admission. He had meticulously filled out all the forms and instructed us not to lose them and to give them to someone in the school office on our first day. The mention of the new school made my stomach tighten, so I helped myself to a second serving of familiarity, or Persian stew.

CHAPTER 3

LAKE TAHOE

Anahita and I weren't going to attend school until after the winter break, which meant we had three weeks to get accustomed to our new home in a foreign country. Farhad suggested that we do some sightseeing before school started. Jasmin lobbied for Lake Tahoe, and we all agreed.

Jasmin drove faster than I liked on the freeways. She seemed almost too comfortable with driving. When she would turn around and glance at Anahita or me to talk to us in the backseat, I would ignore her, hoping she would just turn around and watch the road.

The drive to Lake Tahoe was scenic and reminded me of the drive from Tehran to the Caspian Sea. I was somewhat disappointed that Lake Tahoe was so small compared to the Caspian Sea, but its clear-as-glass surface intrigued me. When my family and I had vacationed at the Caspian Sea, we'd eaten some of the most delicious fish I was ever to eat. I did not realize at the time that it was world famous for its fish and caviar.

Farhad rented us two rooms side by side in one of the casino hotels on the Nevada side of the lake—one for our sisters and one for the two of us. After we checked in and got settled, Farhad announced that he was going down to play his favorite game, roulette.

He was the only one of us who was over twenty-one, so Jasmin took Anahita and me to Denny's for lunch.

"I'm going to get the chocolate cream pie!" Jasmin exclaimed.

Denny's desserts were one of Jasmin's favorite treats. She preferred Denny's over other restaurant chains, as it was affordable and consistent.

While we were waiting for our food to come, Jasmin explained to us that Lake Tahoe was connected to the Pacific Ocean. "If it is, then it wouldn't be a lake," I said. "It would be a bay." We fell into the familiarity of arguing until our food came. Jasmin insisted that she was right, a position she valued almost above everything else. She leaned over and asked the couple dining at the table next to us whether or not the lake was connected to the ocean. They just shrugged and said they didn't know. Jasmin, who had a point to prove, then asked a family sitting on the other side of us. They politely said that they didn't know the answer either. I was surprised that neither group of Americans knew about their own geography and was even more surprised by how apathetic they seemed about knowing. Since Farhad wasn't there to back me up as he usually did and I had no way to prove my point, I decided that, when we got back to San Jose, I would take Jasmin to the public library to prove she was wrong. Jasmin tried to get Anahita to agree with her, but Anahita just looked preoccupied with dipping her french fries into her ketchup and refused to get involved. She was mild tempered and was intimidated by Jasmin's emotional outbursts. Jasmin took advantage of Anahita's feelings of intimidation and sometimes ordered her around like a personal servant.

We walked single file back to the hotel room, as none of us wanted to talk to the others. Our foul mood dissipated as soon as we entered the hotel room and saw Farhad's grin.

"Guess what! I just won two thousand dollars at roulette! Two thousand dollars! Can you believe that?" Farhad exclaimed excitedly. He took the dollar bills out of his wallet, fanned them like playing cards, and fluttered them in our faces.

"What are you going to do with all that money?" Anahita asked.

"I'm going to buy Salma a beautiful ring. She'll be so happy."

Farhad and Salma had recently married. When he spoke of his young wife, his eyes sparkled like the ring he was going to buy.

"That's wasting it. Your wife doesn't need a new ring. You should save it for a house," interjected Jasmin.

Farhad did not let Jasmin's practical advice diminish his excitement. Ignoring her, he described a ring he had seen in a shop window that he knew Salma would love because it had the deep-blue sapphire stones that were her favorite.

The drive back to San Jose was tempered with the knowledge that Farhad would be leaving in a few days to go back to Tehran. Jasmin would be taking care of us by herself. Fortunately, our mother would be coming to visit in the spring, and we hoped to be in a new two-bedroom apartment by then.

We took Farhad to the San Francisco airport on December 30, 1977. Saying good-bye to Farhad and knowing that school would start in just four days was more than Anahita could handle. At the airport, her fears and anxiety came out in streams of tears. She cried as if she would never see Farhad again.

Farhad tenderly hugged her and told her not to worry. "I will come here with Salma soon. You are going to be so busy with school that you won't even notice that I am not here. Don't worry. Everything will be fine."

Driving down US Route 101 after dropping Farhad off at the airport felt different than the last time, when we had just arrived in America. This time I didn't feel like one blip among a million on the longest road ever; I felt as if I were hurling in the fast lane toward an unknown future: starting a new school in a few days with new rules, foreign (to me) kids, and everything in a language I barely understood. Even though I wasn't planning to live in the

United States for the rest of my life and knew that this situation was temporary, just until I finished school, I needed Farhad's reassurance that everything would be okay.

That afternoon, Jasmin took us to a stationery store to get the necessary school supplies. She had attended grades eleven and twelve in San Jose, so she was familiar with school-supplies shopping in the United States. She held the list from Andrew Hill High that Ehsan had given her in one hand while she steered us up and down the aisles, tossing supplies into the basket with her other hand. Most of the items were familiar: pens, notebooks, rulers, and binders. Anahita and I were not familiar with the sports equipment we needed, though, which meant we had to find another store for that. In Iran, we only had to buy plain paper and notebooks. We never used binders, paper clips, or staples in school but did use rulers and other geometry-related supplies.

The week before school started, Anahita and I started going to bed early to prepare for waking up at six thirty each morning. Jasmin would be picking us up in the afternoons after her classes had ended at the community college, but we would have to walk the two or so miles to school in the mornings. That seemed like a long way to me, as I was used to riding the city bus to school in Tehran. Everything here was different, which made me feel the same as when I rode in a boat on the Caspian Sea: that motion sickness feeling where there is no solid ground under my feet.

CHAPTER 4
A NEW YEAR

On New Year's Day 1978, a Saturday morning, Jasmin turned the TV on so Anahita and I could watch a replay of the ball dropping in Times Square, New York City. Since we'd gone to bed early the night before, we'd missed the midnight celebration. The countdown to the New Year sounded like a countdown to school for me. Ten, nine, eight, seven, six, five, four, three, two more days until a brand-new American school. That familiar, sinking feeling in my stomach grew as the crowd in Times Square shouted each number in the countdown. We were about to enter Andrew Hill High School, as second-semester, grade-eleven students. The road to feeling comfortable was based on how good my English was, and right now that road felt full of potholes and puddles. One day, I hoped, it would be as smooth and straight and solid as Highway 101.

We had driven by our new school a couple of weeks ago, but I had no idea what it looked like on the inside nor how it operated. The schools I attended in Iran were usually surrounded by walls, like our homes. Discipline was extremely strict, with no leeway for excuses of any kind. If we students were late to school, we were given a tardy and sent to the principal's office. After three tardies, we were disciplined with a swat on the knuckles or backside with a stick. The assistant principal usually had the pleasure of carrying out that task. We therefore did our best to avoid being disciplined. With such strict control, the teachers never needed to depend on the help of parents to teach their children how to behave in the classroom or remind them to do their homework. Teachers took pride in their charges being compliant and studious.

Monday morning I woke up stiff, as usual, from sleeping on the couch that was a little too short for me. Anahita was already dressed. As we sat down to our usual breakfast of toast and a salty Bulgarian cheese made of sheep's milk, Jasmin smiled and announced that she had found a two-bedroom apartment available for us to move into the beginning of February. "Yay! I won't have to sleep on the couch anymore," I said, relieved, as I stretched my back.

For our first day of school, Jasmin drove us. Andrew Hill High School was much larger than high schools in Iran; it was a massive campus with no walls or huge metal gates. The campus boasted tennis courts, a swimming pool, a track, a soccer field, and a football field. I was overwhelmed by the size of the school. As we walked past a line of pretty cheerleaders practicing their drills, I tried to quickly take in my surroundings to get my bearings.

"Quit staring at those girls, Borz. You should ask them out if you're in love with them," Jasmin shouted.

"No, I'm not in love with them, Jasmin. I was just looking because girls in Iran don't wear such short skirts in school," I stage-whispered, embarrassed.

The universities in Iran were coed, but at the high school and elementary school levels girls and boys were segregated and attended different schools, even during the shah's more relaxed reign. There were plenty of pretty girls in Tehran, but I saw them in the shops and public places, not at school, jumping up and down in skimpy clothes, cheering on boys playing sports.

Anahita and I nervously followed Jasmin to the counselor's office, where she introduced us to Mr. Adams, our counselor. Paunchy and pleasant, Mr. Adams greeted us with a warm smile and showed us into his office. He squeezed between a metal file cabinet and his desk to plop down into his worn desk chair. The desk and the man looked altogether too small for the matchbox-sized, windowless office. Still smiling, he asked us how we were.

"Fine, thank you. How are you?" Anahita and I said in unison.

Mr. Adams laughed. "I see you have learned some English," he said. He then talked to Jasmin, his sentences trotting along at a fast clip.

I strained to understand what he was saying but could recognize only a few words. Jasmin explained that Mr. Adams was going to have a student aide, who was an English learner as well, accompany us to our classes. We waited for the student aide to be paged.

A thin East Indian girl with large, friendly eyes approached us and smiled. "Hi. I'm Meena. I will show you around the school. How are you?"

"Fine, thank you. How are you?" Anahita and I said in unison again. We laughed a little, embarrassed.

Meena did not laugh. She only smiled with a knowing expression. "Don't worry. I will look after you."

"Well, I better get to my classes," Jasmin said and waved goodbye as she hurried down the hall.

I felt much more at ease knowing we had Meena as a guide, a buffer, and possibly our first friend. Meena showed us where the cafeteria, library, and our assigned lockers were. She talked her way through the crowds and past classrooms, but I didn't get most of what she said. She stopped in the doorway of one classroom and said, "This is your first class, US history. I'll be back to take you to your next class when the bell rings and will go with you to all your classes until you get the hang of it. Have fun. See you soon!" She disappeared into the crowd of kids.

Anahita and I looked at each other, wordlessly daring the other to enter the classroom first. I took the dare and walked in.

Most of the other students ignored us. A few paused midsentence to glance over at us and then resumed their conversations. Some students were sitting in desks, and others were standing, talking in small groups. Anahita and I lingered just inside the door, not knowing which desks would be ours.

Just before the tardy bell rang, a bulky man with brown hair and a soft face swooshed into the classroom and dropped his worn leather briefcase onto the desk, sending all the standing students scrambling to their seats. His facial expression engendered trust and made him seem like someone we had known for years.

"Welcome back to class, everyone. I hope you had a good break and got some rest. You'll need it, because we are going to go hard and fast this semester."

Just then, he noticed us standing by the door. "Looks like we have a couple of new students. Welcome! I am Mr. Stevens. You must be the foreign exchange students," he said as he scanned the classroom. "There are two empty desks in the second row toward the back. Please sit there." If he had not pointed to the two empty desks, I don't think Anahita and I would have known what he was saying. We quickly took our seats.

I had never encountered a teacher as friendly as Mr. Stevens in Iran.

"Class, this is Anahita and Borz Alikhani. They have come all the way from Iran to study at our school. Can anyone tell me where Iran is?" He picked up a piece of chalk and wrote *Iran* on the board, simultaneously saying the word out loud. He pronounced it "I-ran," which made Anahita and me giggle.

"How fast you run?" I asked aloud. Everyone laughed.

"How do you pronounce the name of your country, then?" Mr. Stevens asked.

I did not know what *pronounce* meant but assumed it meant to read again, so I slowly said, "Ee-rawn."

"Where is Ee-rawn?" a boy sitting in the front row asked.

"Earth," I answered, which brought another round of laughter from the class.

Mr. Stevens walked over to a large, stiff world map hanging from a wooden roller on the wall and pointed to Iran. A girl sitting next to me shouted, "You border Russia!" I immediately understood what *border* meant. I was actually learning new vocabulary by listening to everyone. Within a couple of short minutes I had mastered the words *pronounce* and *border*. A wave of relief washed over me. Being in this foreign school wasn't going to be as hard as I'd thought. But then the lecture began. I turned around to look at Anahita, and her expression mirrored what I was feeling: lost and overwhelmed. I smiled at her, to let her know that it would all be okay.

When the bell rang, Meena came as she had promised and led us to our second class, which was English as a second language.

"I used to be in this class but graduated out of it because my English is good enough now to be in regular English language arts classes. The teacher is Mr. Brown. You are going to love him. He will teach you English in no time," Meena explained. "Whatever you do, don't touch his keys," she warned as she turned around and disappeared into the crowded hallway.

Mr. Brown's class was full of foreign students, mostly from Mexico. There were a handful of East Indian kids and two Iranian boys. One of them approached Anahita right away and tried to flirt with her. She gave him a look so smoldering with disdain that he never approached her again. I had not known she was capable of such looks but was glad to see she could fend for herself.

Mr. Brown was a patient man devoted to his students and his craft of teaching ESL. He had taught English to foreign students for over thirty years and never seemed to tire of helping yet another student with the rudimentary beginnings of learning vocabulary, tenses, and articles. As he probably had when he'd first started out teaching, he had the class learn a silly song to understand the difference between *at, in,* and *on:*

> There is a hole *at* the bottom of the sea, there is a hole at the bottom of the sea. There is a hole, there is a hole, there is a hole at the bottom of the sea.
>
> There is a log *in* the hole at the bottom of the sea, there is a log in the hole at the bottom of the sea. There is a log, there is a log, there is a log in the hole at the bottom of the sea.
>
> There is a frog *on* the log in the hole at the bottom of the sea, there is a frog on the log in the hole at the bottom of the sea. There is a frog, there is a frog, there is a frog on the log in the hole at the bottom of the sea.

The song became totally confusing when he added a flea on the frog on the log in a hole at the bottom of the sea, but it was a fun way to learn.

Just before class was to be dismissed, Anahita asked me in Farsi, "What did Meena mean about Mr. Brown's keys?" I shrugged. I had no idea.

When Meena came to pick us up, I asked her, "What about Mr. Brown's keys?"

She laughed and said, "You'll see."

After the final bell of the day rang, Anahita and I went to Mr. Brown's office to ask for some clarification on one of his assignments. As we walked in, he was cleaning his ear with one of his keys. When he took it out, there was a gross blob of wax on the end of it. Now I knew what Meena meant. I wondered how he hadn't gone deaf from this habit.

Jasmin was parked out front waiting for us when school dismissed for the day at three o'clock. She peppered us with questions the whole way home. As soon as we got in the door, she said, "You better start your homework. I don't want you getting behind. Father didn't send you all the way here to slack off."

Anahita and I sat at the kitchen table and started with math homework. It was way too easy for us, and we finished it in ten minutes. History, on the other hand, took us hours to complete. Anahita and I had been allowed to take the history textbook home so we could read the chapter that Mr. Stevens had lectured on. We looked up every word we didn't know in our English-Farsi dictionary and wrote the meaning of the word above it. There was a test in a week on the chapter, which was about the Civil War, so we divided it into equal chunks by the number of days we had until the test and studied like this for a couple of hours each night. Both of us were determined and motivated to learn and keep up with our peers, and I had a special interest in history. Each day, our progress accelerated as our vocabulary grew. By the time we had our first quiz, I had learned not only a lot of English vocabulary but also some of the dark history of the American Civil War.

CHAPTER 5
GRADES

On Saturday morning my sisters and I went to see the new apartment. After the elderly property manager unlocked the door, I ran inside to confirm that there were two bedrooms. There were not only two bedrooms but also two bathrooms. No more sharing a small bathroom made even smaller with a multitude of makeup and hair products littering the countertop.

Jasmin tempered my excitement when she began questioning the property manager. "This dishwasher looks old. Are you sure it works? The counter is coming up on this corner. Will it be fixed? Are you going to have the carpets cleaned?"

Anahita seemed neutral. She and Jasmin would share the larger bedroom and the bathroom that was attached to it.

"Let's go see what the pool looks like," Anahita said.

The apartment building was older than our current complex, but the pool and recreation area were larger. I was sold.

Later that day, after we'd returned home, Mom called to say she would be visiting us in two or three months. We were all excited, especially Anahita, who immediately began preparing for Mom's visit. She wrote out a list of all the things we would show Mom when she came. Mom would arrive right after Nowruz, or "New

Day," which is the Persian New Year. All Persians around the world celebrate Nowruz at the exact same time. Since the Persian community was practically nonexistent where we lived, we could not get a hold of a Persian calendar to know precisely when Nowruz would take place. We knew it fell between March 19 and 22 but did not know the exact time this year. We toyed with the idea of going to the library, but none of us wanted to put in that much effort. Thinking of Mom made me homesick for her cooking and for Persian culture in general. I also missed the smell of her cigarettes. I could not conjure up an image in my mind of Mom without smelling her cigarettes.

Anahita and I adjusted to the routine of school and homework. All our classes were the same except for math and PE. I was in Algebra II, and Anahita had geometry. I took swimming, and she signed up for softball. I thought I would be getting off easy taking swimming, since I knew how to swim, but was shocked when I saw the size of the pool. It was much larger than any pool I had swum in back home. The PE coach didn't make things easy for me or anyone. His dictatorial attitude made me nervous. Anahita struggled with trying to fit in on the softball team. In some ways, the physical classes were harder than the academic classes. It took a few weeks, but we soon got the routines down and were able to adjust. We caught on to the academics quickly, never scoring less than 90 percent on any exam or quiz. My PE grade was my lowest grade until a friend named Scott showed me how to swim faster. Using his techniques helped me get my PE grade up over 90 percent like all my other grades. In exchange for Scott showing me how to swim faster, I helped him with his math homework. Soon word spread, and I began tutoring a number of kids in math.

Tutoring math didn't require me to be fluent in English, because math is a universal language. I therefore wasn't nervous about helping my classmates. All I had to do was show them with pencil and paper how to solve a problem. Answering their questions, though, helped me to improve my English.

Shortly after starting classes at Andrew Hill, I became aware of how large the achievement gap was between the schools in the United States and the ones I attended in Iran. In my old country, we studied calculus in the tenth grade, and now I was retaking Algebra II in eleventh grade. Math and science classes in Iran were rigorous, but we never had a chance to do lab work, because such labs didn't exist in the high schools. In the United States, though, kids had the opportunity to run experiments in well-stocked labs before they ever got to college.

The universities in Iran, however, were inferior to the ones in the United States. They had high standards of achievement but offered few courses. They accepted the majority of students who could pass the entry exams, which were so difficult that rumor had it they had been designed for failure since there were very few spaces at the university for new students. Many students had to wait years to get into the local universities after they passed the entry exams. For these reasons, Iranian students who had the means preferred to get their degrees in the United States or Europe. Many Iranian families in the 1970s, including my own, chose to send their kids abroad to finish the last two years of high school overseas so that they could learn the language before entering college.

Anahita, Jasmin, and I moved into the new apartment on February 1. Ehsan rented a small U-Haul truck to help us transport our personal belongings. We didn't need to move any of the furniture, because Jasmin had rented it all from a furniture rental store for eighteen dollars a month. The two-bedroom apartment would cost us thirty-six dollars a month to furnish. The furniture store brought over brand-new furniture for our new place. Jasmin was pleased. "Wow! I just had to make one simple phone call, and the rental company arranged to pick up the furniture at our old place and deliver brand-new furniture here," she said. "Things that are so complicated in Iran are so much easier here. I called PG&E, and they are disconnecting the gas and electric at the old place and have already turned it on here. Amazing! In Iran it would take weeks to cancel service at one place and years to start it in another."

I was impressed with how easily my sister managed the business of living. She was only two years older than me, but she seemed to have grown up so much since she'd left Tehran a couple of years ago. I wondered if I would grow up that fast too, being in America.

Jasmin had come to the United States to study psychology. She planned to become a psychologist and go back to Tehran to practice. Whenever she drove anywhere, she would comment on the driving skills of others. She would say that although the American drivers were "crazy," as she put it, they weren't as crazy as the drivers in Iran.

"Look at that crazy guy acting like he owns the whole road," Jasmin would point out as she slowed down to let a driver weave between her and a truck two car lengths ahead. "He's as crazy as drivers back home. When I become a psychologist, I'm going to get at the root of why people insist on putting everyone else's lives in danger when they drive. Do you remember, Borz, how people drive up on the curbs to pass slow cars on the main street near our house? And do you remember how much people honk back home? That is all pent-up anger. Everyone back home seems angry about something. Or sad. I'm sick and tired of hearing the gloomy, melancholic songs that are so popular now coming out of Iran. What's wrong with everyone? There are so many people who will need my service when I get back!"

Whenever Jasmin went on about how important she would be as a psychologist back home, I remembered what Dad had said to me once about the general gloomy attitude of Persians. I kept his comments to myself, though, as I did not want to burst her bubble and start another argument. Dad claimed that before Persia had been invaded by the wandering tribes of Arabs, Mongols, and

Turks, the Persians had been a content people and had held elaborate celebrations for holidays of both little and large importance.

The new apartment was in the same neighborhood as our old apartment but a little closer to our school, which was about a mile and a half away. I quickly got accustomed to the cool morning walks to contemplate my upcoming classes. Jasmin picked us up from school on Wednesdays and Fridays, and we walked home the other days. Sometimes Anahita and I would quiz each other with vocabulary words on our walks home. We were both determined to conquer the language barrier.

When April came, our apartment took on a new energy as we waited for Mom to fly in on the tenth. Jasmin ordered Anahita to clean the apartment as if the shah himself was arriving. She nagged us constantly to put away our books and notebooks, which seemed to migrate out of our backpacks on their own. We helped her shop for more groceries than would reasonably fit in the small kitchen and lamented the fact that there was no Persian market anywhere to buy the spices and other things we sorely missed.

The day before Mom's arrival, Anahita stopped at a nursery on the way back from school and picked up a multicolored bouquet of flowers to give to her when she arrived. As we were sitting down to dinner in our now-spotless kitchen, Dad called to say that Mom wouldn't be coming until April 15, five days later. Anahita looked crestfallen.

"It's better that way, Anahita," I said. "Now Mom will arrive on Saturday instead of Monday. We won't have to take a day off school to pick her up at the airport in San Francisco, and we can plan to get all our homework done by Friday night so we have the whole weekend to spend with her without having homework harass us."

Anahita gave me the smiling-mouth, sad-eyes look that I had seen on her many times before.

Monday started out extraordinarily ordinary. Instead of missing school to pick up Mom at the airport, Anahita and I were now sitting in our classes. The only thing that broke the standard routine of the day was the boy and girl in the back of history class who started making out in the middle of the lecture. It was distracting to the whole class except Mr. Stevens, who droned on and on, as if nothing was awry, about the proposed amendment to the Constitution to free the slaves and assure equal protection under the law for all Americans. I turned around to look at Anahita. She was busily taking notes, but her cheeks were blush red. This kind of behavior was never tolerated in our schools back home.

The next day, report cards were passed out during first period. I got all As except for PE class, in which I got an A minus. Anahita received all A minuses except for one A. We were called into the principal's office during recess. Anahita and I tentatively stepped into the waiting area, where the receptionist greeted us in her everyday sunny voice. Here we were, probably in trouble, yet Mrs. Johnson was acting as if nothing was wrong. I resented her for being what I thought was two-faced.

Mr. Rogerson, the principal, opened the door to his inner office and asked us to come in and sit down. We sat down in front of his large, shiny desk, sitting straight up and at attention. Anahita looked down at her fidgeting hands, but I looked straight at Mr. Rogerson as he took a seat across the desk from us. He always dressed in an impeccable suit, and today it was the same gray as his neatly combed hair. As he started to talk in his silky voice, I imagined I was talking to the president of the United States. He picked up two papers from the top of a neat pile and looked me straight in the eye and smiled.

"I want to congratulate you both, Anahita and Borz, for being the top two students at Andrew Hill High! Borz, you might have the top grades in the whole school district. Remarkable! By your grades, I see that you are probably helping Anahita, but I have to admit that I thought it was the other way around; I thought Anahita would get higher grades than you. I was wrong." He chuckled.

As we walked past the receptionist on our way out, I gave her a big smile, in part because I was ecstatic with the news of our grades and also to make up for prematurely judging her as two-faced.

"Mom is going to be so proud," Anahita said, skipping ahead of me on our way home.

"Jasmin will probably be jealous," I replied, and we both laughed.

Jasmin walked in the door at six that evening. Anahita and I excitedly ran to greet her to tell her about our report card, but the foul look on her face evaporated our feelings of joy.

"Stupid old lady! I'm trying to get home after a long day, and this stupid old lady was driving twenty-five in a forty-five-mile-per-hour zone. I couldn't pass for blocks! It should be illegal to drive after fifty years old." She slammed the door and threw down her bags.

"What are you two standing there for?" she asked.

I spoke first. "Anahita and I got our report cards."

"Look," Anahita said as she handed them to our big sister. "Mr. Rogerson said that we got the top grades in the whole school, maybe in the whole district."

"Wow. That's great! Let's go to Denny's for dinner to celebrate. I love their burgers," Jasmin said. Anahita and I were overjoyed.

"But remember, Anahita," Jasmin said, "orange juice upsets my ulcers, so don't let me order it, okay?"

When we arrived at Denny's, the hostess showed us to a booth and asked if we would like anything to drink.

"May I have a small orange juice, please?" Jasmin asked the hostess.

"No, Jasmin, don't order that," Anahita jumped in. "Remember, orange juice isn't good for your ulcers."

"Are you going to tell me what I can and cannot order? I'll order what I want. You don't know anything," Jasmin said.

"You're psycho, Jasmin!" I said disgustedly. "You say one thing, then deny you ever said it. You need a shrink!"

The hostess left us to sort out our family matters ourselves.

"That's how you treat me? After all I have done for you two? I break my back trying to go to school, take care of the apartment, pay the bills, make sure you are fed and do your homework, and pick you up from school. You, Anahita, sit there and try to deny me one small glass of orange juice, while you, Borz, call me crazy. I'm going to let Mom know what ingrates you both are."

"I can't wait until Mom comes, so she can see how you treat us, especially Anahita," I whisper-shouted.

Jasmin glared at me and was about to argue some more, but then the waitress returned to take our order. Jasmin pulled her lips into a fake smile and ordered a hamburger and small orange juice. I counted the days until Mom would arrive.

CHAPTER 6
THERE SHE IS

I woke up Saturday morning to Anahita singing a popular Persian song as she put away the dishes. I jumped out of bed, excited to get ready to go to San Francisco International Airport to pick up Mom. We left at ten thirty in the morning to make sure we had enough time to park and get to the exit where foreigners emerge after passing through immigration and customs. Mom was coming in on Alitalia Airlines from Rome. Before we left our apartment, Jasmin called Alitalia Airlines several times to see if the plane was arriving on time, but no one picked up the phone on the other end. Exasperatedly, Jasmin slammed the phone down, stormed out of the house, and started the car without waiting for Anahita and me to get in.

When we arrived at the airport and checked the monitor, all three of us let out a collective groan, as Mom's flight had been delayed three hours. An old Iranian lady who was checking the monitor at the same time turned toward us and told us that Alitalia is always late, shouting the word *always*. We smiled through our frustration and nodded in agreement. Jasmin marched off, finding a seat near the window. Staring out the window, she silently fumed.

"Let's just sit over here, Anahita. Just pretend Jasmin isn't even here," I said, leading Anahita to a row of seats as far from Jasmin as we could get without losing sight of her.

At three o'clock, Jasmin got up and walked over to Mom's gate. We followed her from a safe distance. After a half hour of watching people emerge and happily unite with family and friends, Jasmin screamed. She had spotted Mom. I followed her gaze and found Mom in the crowd, walking toward us.

"There she is! There she is!" Anahita shouted. "Look at her beautiful purple dress!" Although short, Mom looked like a movie star. Her dark-blonde hair, light skin, and green eyes made her look more French or Italian. Our friends back home always commented on how pretty our mother was.

Mom tried to run toward us the second she spotted the three of us waving and jumping up and down in the crowd, but her two enormous suitcases held her down. Seconds later, she dropped the suitcases and wrapped her arms around us, planting kisses on each of our cheeks. Mom's familiar scent of perfume and cigarette smoke enveloped us in the embrace. I hadn't been this happy for months. Anahita was crying out of happiness, and even Jasmin was grinning excitedly.

"My darlings. I brought you many bags of Persian pistachios. I also picked up some shirts and shoes and dresses in Rome for all of you. My bags are so heavy with gifts that I'm surprised they let me on the plane. Borz, you have gotten so tall! You can carry the suitcases."

Now we knew why Mom was five days late. She had taken the opportunity to shop in Rome. It was typical of Dad to give us just the briefest of information and not go into any details. His minimalist way of communicating was a source of collective frustration for the rest of the family.

The drive home was completely unlike the ride up to the airport. Jasmin was happier than I had seen her since we had arrived.

There was none of the usual tension. It was like we were all on holiday, even though it was just Mom who was vacationing.

As Mom rolled down her window a couple of inches to let her cigarette smoke escape, she told us that Iran was chaotic these days. She said that antigovernment activists were protesting against the shah. Martial law hadn't been declared, but arson and destruction were happening in some areas of Tehran. She and Dad weren't worried, though, because they believed the government would be able to control the unrest. Dad's restaurant business was as busy as usual.

In Iran, we would eat at Dad's fancy restaurant on weekends, and at home we had a housemaid who washed the dishes and cleaned the house. A lot of households in our neighborhood hired cooks, but my mom never allowed anyone else to cook for us, because nobody could beat her skills in the kitchen. She made the best Persian and European dishes.

When we got home, Mom filled us in on all the news about our cousins, aunts, and uncles. There had been no deaths or marriages in the family, so everything was much as we had left it.

Anahita and I told Mom about our grades and how well we had adjusted to school.

"That's wonderful, kids. Since you are doing so well, let's plan a trip this summer. Dad gave me eight thousand dollars, and he is depositing another twenty-five thousand in your account, Jasmin, so we will not want for anything. I want to see Las Vegas and Los Angeles as well as other places while I'm here."

I was so excited to be reunited with Mom and to be able to go to these places with her. It was going to be a summer worth remembering.

Mom called Dad to let him know that she had arrived safely and that all of us were doing well. She asked how he and Farhad were and if the streets were still in an upheaval with the protesters. Dad assured her that everything had been calm since she had left and that things were fine at our family's restaurant. Dad owned two primary businesses. One was a catering company called Food Service that catered only to the royal family. He also owned one of the largest and nicest restaurants in Tehran. It was in a massive two-story brick building, with about thirty thousand square feet of space, located in the nice part of town. It was furnished with high-end tables and chairs. Crystal chandeliers hung from the ceilings. The waitstaff were seasoned servers who knew how to cater to the loyal patrons. The restaurant served gourmet Persian and European food.

When she hung up the phone, Mom opened her large black suitcases and pulled out a giant bag of Persian pistachios. To me, they were like candy. Their distinctive flavor took me back to my life in Tehran, where I'd eaten them every day on my way home from school, tossing the shells behind me like a trail of breadcrumbs that led from school, onto the bus, and to home. Mom probed around in her suitcases and passed out presents.

"Borz, look, I got you nice leather shoes from Rome," Mom said, handing me a bag with a fancy Italian name on it. I opened the bag and was delighted with the orange shoes made from the softest leather I had ever felt. Turning them over in my hands, I could not believe that something as practical as a pair of shoes could be a masterpiece of design. I kept those shoes for thirty years.

Ehsan called that night to talk to Mom and to invite us to dinner next Saturday. His wife, Mahshid, was going to make a traditional Persian feast. Ehsan's cousin Nassir, who was also Mahshid's first cousin, and some of their friends were also invited.

Saturday evening we all drove to Ehsan's apartment. Nassir greeted us at the door and ushered us into the small but well-furnished apartment.

"Welcome, welcome!" Ehsan said. "So nice to see you, Mrs. Alikhani. I hope you had a good flight."

Nassir introduced us to Thuy, his American-born Chinese girlfriend. She was petite, with a pretty face. Nassir looked more

African than many Iranians, with his darker skin, brown eyes, and thick, kinky hair. Iran, like the United States, has always been a melting pot of different ethnicity, including Persians (or Aryans), Turks, Mongols, Balochis, Kurds (who are also Aryan), and Arabs (whose Saudi version is close to Africans). Unlike the United States, though, it does not matter what one's original race or ethnicity is; we are all Iranian with one common language. No legal forms in Iran ask about race or ethnicity, unlike those in the United States.

For the past 2,500 years, Iran has kept a written record of its history, where one can read about the entrance of the different races and tribes that took up residence in Persia. The country had always been called Persia until, out of respect for the many different races that comprise the country, Reza Shah, the father of the late Shah Mohammad Reza Pahlavi, renamed the country Iran. With such a diverse population, an Iranian could have characteristics ranging from dark African to white European.

In the United States, Nassir was frequently mistaken for black, or African American. He would respond that he was pure Iranian, earning him confused looks. It did not bother him that he looked more African than what many assumed Iranians looked like. He never made anyone uncomfortable for guessing wrongly what his background was, as he had a knack for turning an awkward situation into a joke.

The smells wafting from the kitchen were almost too tantalizing to take. I tried to wander in to sneak a sample, but Mom and Mahshid shooed me out before I could dip a spoon into a pot. Between Mom's cooking and Mahshid's feast, I felt as if I were back in my motherland again. When dinner was finally served, I crowded my plate with lamb kebabs, Persian rice, roasted eggplant, and salad.

After dinner, Mahshid, Mom, and my sisters cleared the dishes and started dancing. I joined the men in the living room with their tea. Politics, as usual, dominated the conversation. Ehsan started talking about the uprisings in Iran. He proclaimed that things were much worse than what was being reported, that people were demanding that the shah step down. He said that he wanted the shah to go, but I could not understand why. His dad was a millionaire who had made his fortune during the shah's regime. The ugly reality that I was beginning to realize was that ordinary people hated the shah, the man my father said had given Iran the modern world as we had never before experienced.

"Iranians are never thankful for what they have," Nassir interjected. "They are always critical of whoever the current ruler is and suspicious of what they do, even if it benefits the country. I agree that Pahlavi's government has its shortcomings, but prior to Reza Shah's reign, Iran was a medieval society under the Qajar dynasty, whose kings, as you probably remember from history class, were the descendants of the nomadic Turkish tribes that invaded Iran. I'm glad I'm here where I don't have to deal with all the conflict everyone over there is drumming up. What's wrong with trying to see the glass half full?"

As the conversation heated up, I stood up and asked, "What do the protestors want? Who do they want to bring to power? Who is their leader?"

"The shah may have to step down and leave," Ehsan said. "Ayatollah Khomeini may emerge as the leader of the protestors, which means that this mullah may lead Iran!" Ehsan said disdainfully.

Oh my god! Khomeini! I thought. *Khomeini, Khomeini, Khomeini ... where have I heard that name before?* The sound of it brought a feeling of fear over me. I was immediately transported back to when I was thirteen years old, in 1974, riding the bus home from school. We had just moved to a more affluent part of Tehran in the middle of the school year. I had to take a city bus from our new house to my old school, which was about eight miles away. When the new school year started, I could transfer to the closer school near our new home. I was sitting on the bus on the window side of the seat. I looked down and saw that someone had scribbled "Khomeini" with a black marker on the wall, under the window. It was small, but something about the way the word was scribbled caught my eye and captured my attention. It was somewhat hidden but still seemed to radiate a power of its own.

When I got home, I found my mom in the kitchen, stirring a large pot of stew. I asked her who Khomeini was.

She stopped stirring and turned to face me with angry red cheeks. "Who told you this name?" she demanded.

"I saw it on the bus. Someone had written it on the wall under the window where I was sitting." I didn't know why I felt so defensive, but Mom's tone made me feel as if I had done something wrong.

"Don't ever mention that criminal's name again! He is against the government and was exiled by the regime back in the 1960s. If your father hears you speak that name, he will be very angry."

The next day, I asked my teacher who Khomeini was. His eyes got wide, and he stopped in midstride as he was crossing the classroom. He turned toward me and told me to go to the office. They kept me there until my father came to pick me up.

When Dad came into the office, he was visibly upset. It confused me that one name could cause so many dark feelings, but I did not want to approach the subject with my father until he brought it up. Mom had asked me not to utter the name, so I knew I would be in trouble for that, but what was behind the name? The way people recoiled at the mention of it only piqued my curiosity more.

On the way home, Dad took a deep breath and recounted some history so I could better understand who Khomeini was. He said that Khomeini was an ayatollah, a Shiite religious leader, who had been deported to Iraq for trying to spark an uprising against the shah. Although Dad knew history better than anyone in our family, he did not know exactly what Khomeini wanted, because the shah did not allow the clergy to speak freely in public. Dad explained that the shah, like any other human being, wasn't perfect and that his sense of insecurity was a major weakness. The shah was afraid that if someone spoke out against him, there could be an uprising in the country, resulting in a change of government. Dad went on to say that the shah's fear of uprisings and chaos forced him to control the media and not respect freedom of speech. Dad explained that Khomeini had been deported after inciting uprisings in the holy city of Qom. Khomeini had spoken harshly against the regime and called on Iranian Muslims to overthrow the government, which of course threatened the shah. As we got closer to home, Dad concluded by telling me that with Khomeini now living outside of Iran in Turkey, Iraq, and France and with the shah and the clergy keeping the whole situation as secret as they could, Khomeini had become a mysterious man that drew a lot of people to him. No one knew what, exactly, this mysterious man had against the regime. People, I realized, were afraid to even utter Khomeini's name because of the shah's secret police, SAVAK, which imposed the anti-free-speech regulations the shah had ordered.

As we walked up the street to our house, I promised my father that I would never mention the name again.

But in Ehsan's living room, the forbidden word peppered the conversation, evoking either anger or arguments. It was 1978, and the name Khomeini began popping up pell-mell throughout American news reports. He was all over the news openly asking the Iranian people to rise up and oust the shah. Journalists supported Khomeini's cause by showing photos of people tortured by the regime. To add fire to the flame, talk shows reminded their listeners that the shah had raised the price of crude oil often enough to affect England's, America's, and other countries' economies.

Toward the end of the evening, as guests gathered their jackets and purses, I quietly asked Ehsan, "Can the shah's regime control the situation? Will they be able to stop the uprisings?"

"I'm not sure, Borz. We'll see. I follow the Iranian news as much as the American news, and what I hear from Tehran, it is discouraging."

I wondered what would happen to my family and our businesses in Tehran. We were living a comfortable life. My dad had two successful businesses, several homes, and a plot of land. What would happen to everything? If the revolutionaries seized power, would my dad get in trouble because his catering company only catered to the shah? Although the men had talked many hours about the what-ifs, I left feeling anxious for my family. There were so many unanswered questions and uncertainties that took up residence in the hearts of every Iranian I knew.

CHAPTER 7
LAKE TAHOE AGAIN

On the drive home, Mom announced that our relatives Gita and her son, Changiz, were going to visit us from Minnesota when school got out and come with us on our trips to Lake Tahoe and Los Angeles. Gita and her husband, Keyvan, were from good families. Keyvan had been an engineer in Tehran before moving to the United States. Gita's great-grandfather and my mom's great-grandfather had been brothers. Gita was a beautiful woman, with deep-black hair, fair skin, and green eyes. She was taller than most of the women in my family and looked more Parisian than Persian. She dressed well to enhance her innate beauty. Gita prided herself on her looks and sometimes treated others with disrespect, whether knowingly or not. We were all looking forward to their visit and were blissfully unaware of the water-and-oil combination that Gita's and Jasmin's personalities would be.

The last two weeks of school were a breeze for Anahita and me. Each day we would come home to Mom in the kitchen, dishing up a delicious plate of Persian snacks for us. We were looking forward to Gita and Changiz arriving the day after school got out, and we both were expecting to get straight As on our report cards. There was only one dark cloud on our horizon, and that was the news coming out of Tehran.

ABC and NBC nightly news programs showed the demonstrations in Tehran every night with the protestors chanting, "Death to the shah!" It looked as if the army was keeping order, but we couldn't be sure. Mom called Dad one evening to ask him about the situation there. He reassured her that things were okay. He thought things would cool off when people got tired of demonstrating. I was consoled by Dad's words, but Mom was not. She decided to cut her visit short and return to Iran in July or sooner, instead of at the end of August, as she had originally planned.

The last day of school wasn't much different than any of the other days. Anahita and I returned our books, shook our teachers' hands, said good-bye to our friends, and went home. Our original plan had been to take some classes in the summer to make up for the first semester of eleventh grade that we had missed while waiting to get our visas in Tehran, but with our Lake Tahoe and Los Angeles trips already planned, we decided to wait until the last half of summer to make up the classes. Our counselor confirmed that it was okay to take the extra-credit classes later in the summer. This made Anahita and me very happy. Now we could go on our summer vacations and have fun.

The Saturday after school let out, we all went to the airport to pick up Gita and Changiz. As Gita approached us, I could not help but notice how beautiful she was for a mom. Even though she was in her forties, she turned heads, including mine. She wore an emerald-colored dress that matched her unusual green eyes. She gave Mom and my sisters kisses on both cheeks and put out her hand to shake mine. I clumsily took it, secretly wishing we could have kissed cheeks instead.

Her son, Changiz, had not inherited her beauty. He was a year older than me, was chubby, and displayed a bad case of acne. I hoped he wouldn't use my towel when we got home. Regardless of his looks, I enjoyed his company. He constantly cracked jokes, was full of playful energy, and always devised ways to have fun. He reminded me a little of Nassir.

The drive home was a preview of things to come as the rift between Jasmin and Gita began to form. Mom was aware of the small darts flying back and forth between my sister and Gita. The darts were tiny put-downs and not anything to worry too much about, or at least that was how Mom handled it. She kept smiling, hoping that these underhanded comments would be the only weapons Jasmin and Gita would throw. Little did Anahita and I know that these two conceited women were on a collision course of clashing egos. Both carried themselves a little above everyone else. The problem seemed to be that each of them felt that there was only room at the top for one of them.

When we pulled up to the apartment, my mom asked Changiz and me to carry the luggage in. "I would have brought more stuff, but my sleeping bag took up half my suitcase," Changiz told me as we heaved the heavy bags out of the trunk. Relief washed over me when he mentioned his sleeping bag. It turned my stomach to think I would have to share any bedding with Changiz and his pimply face and neck. The drive back from the airport had given me ample time to think of a safe place to store my towel and shaver.

Mom, Gita, and my sisters had already decided on the sleeping arrangements by the time Changiz and I came in with the suitcases. Mom and Gita would share one of the bedrooms, Jasmin and Anahita would take the other one, and Changiz and I were relegated to the couches in the living room. I was on the couch again. Changiz opened his suitcase, withdrew his sleeping bag, and rolled it out on the longer of the two couches, claiming it as his own. Being that he was six feet tall and probably weighed over two hundred pounds, it only made sense that he would have the longer couch. In stature, he lived up to the historical reference of his name but not in temperament, which was playful and friendly.

Changiz is the Farsi pronunciation of Genghis, as in Genghis Khan, the Mongolian warrior who overthrew and destroyed the Persian civilization in 1219. Genghis Khan, a merciless conqueror, burned our homes, cities, and libraries to the ground. I wondered why Changiz's parents had given their son such a dreadful name. I have never met a Brit named Napoleon nor a Jew named Adolf. I could not and still cannot understand why Persians name their babies after such a barbarian.

The next day, we all piled back into the Toyota, Tahoe bound. With Changiz being the largest, he got to sit in the passenger seat. Gita, Mom, Anahita, and I crammed into the backseat. My slender sister sat on one side of me and Gita on the other.

Gita wore her beauty like a badge. It defined her. And because few possessed the elegance and attractiveness that she had, she held herself above everyone else. Her posture was impeccable, which emphasized the way she looked down on everyone. Having the honor of sitting not just next to her but squished up against her was thrilling.

After driving for a couple of hours, Gita asked if we could stop at McDonald's for lunch. We pulled into a McDonald's parking lot and tumbled out of the car. Mom immediately lit a cigarette. Gita went ahead inside, not waiting to see if we were all together or not. Jasmin shot Mom a glance of disapproval at what, to her, was unacceptably rude behavior. When we got in line at the counter, Gita was already ordering herself a Big Mac and fries. Mom bought lunch for Changiz and the rest of us. By the time we ordered, Gita was sitting at a table alone, eating her meal. In Iran, it was customary to ask your relatives what they wanted to eat before ordering your own food. Gita's audaciously arrogant attitude set off Jasmin. Jasmin tipped her head in her haughty manner at Mom, silently imploring her to do something about Gita's poor manners. Mom ignored Jasmin, and we all sat down and ate our burgers at a table on the other side of the small restaurant from Gita. By the time we were done and walking back to the car, Gita was standing in the shade of a tree, waiting for us. Without looking at her, Jasmin got in the car and started it up. Changiz and I were engrossed in a conversation comparing American girls to Iranian girls and were not bothered by Gita's odd behavior. Gita's beauty had cast a spell over me, so I could not see any fault in her actions. Changiz was used to his mom and her behavior.

We arrived in South Lake Tahoe in the late afternoon. The sun split the lake into a thousand splinters of light. Shadows shaded the mountains dark as the sun lowered into the red skirts of clouds beneath it. Mom asked Jasmin to pull over somewhere so we could watch the sunset, but Jasmin was in a fury about the lunch incident and in too much of a hurry to get to the hotel.

Jasmin squealed the car's tires as she squeezed into a parking space at the Sahara Tahoe Casino, one of the best hotels and casinos in the area, majestically situated on Lake Tahoe's popular south shore. We checked in and got two side-by-side lake-view rooms. Mesmerized by the view, Anahita had to be coerced from the window to join us for dinner.

Gita had changed into a pale-green dress of lightweight, flowing material. Jasmin had also changed, into a white summer dress. When they encountered each other in the hall outside our rooms, each looked down the slope of her nose, summing up the other's outfit.

Mom, as usual, tried to make light of the situation. "Gita and Jasmin, you both look gorgeous," she said.

The silence in the elevator as we descended to the main floor made me feel very uncomfortable. I knew it was because of Jasmin and Gita, who by now were outwardly resentful of each other. The elevator opened onto the casino floor.

"Oh, blackjack," Gila exclaimed as she noticed the tables. "I love to play blackjack, and I am very good at it. But I'm only good at it if no one is watching me. I'm going to play a little. Go on; I'll catch up with you later. Let's meet at the restaurant at eight."

"Fine, Gita," Mom conceded. "I'll take the children over to the gift shops. See you at eight."

Before Mom had finished talking, Gita had already sat down at one of the half-moon tables, smiling at the dealer and withdrawing her leather wallet from her oversize handbag.

"How can you let her run everything?" Jasmin demanded of Mom. "She acts like this is her trip and her trip alone. I was the one that got us here. If it weren't for me and my car, there wouldn't even be a vacation. She shows me—us—no respect and does only exactly what she wants. I can't stand being with her."

No one felt much in the mood for shopping, except for Changiz, who chose to wander around the shops. The rest of us headed back to our room. Jasmin lectured Mom all the way back up in the elevator, as if Gita's behavior were Mom's fault. When we got to the room, Anahita went straight to the picture window, tuning out Jasmin.

Jasmin marched over to her suitcase and threw all the clothes she had strewn on the bed back into it.

"What are you doing?" Mom asked.

"I'm leaving. I'm going back to San Jose. I can't spend another minute with that woman and her snobby, snooty ways."

"What!" Mom and I shouted in unison.

"You can't do that, Jasmin," Mom said. "It's dark out. You can't drive down the mountain roads in the dark. There are no lights, and there are lots of sharp turns. The side of the road drops off thousands of feet. It's just too dangerous.

"And what about us? Are you planning on leaving your sister and brother and me stuck here too? What's got into you?"

"What's got into *me*? What do you mean what's got into me? Nothing's got into me. It's her! Don't you see how she looks down on me? And it's not just me. It's all of you too, but you guys are just blind to it. Or stupid. I don't know which. How can you let her do exactly what she wants without considering us at all? She acts like the queen! How come you don't stand up for me when she gives me those looks, Mom? Don't worry about me. As if you ever did. I'm fine driving by myself. I got us up here, didn't I?"

Jasmin went into the bathroom and slammed the door. Mom, Anahita, and I looked at each other in disbelief. Would Jasmin really leave us? I hoped that when the bathroom door opened, a sane, calm Jasmin would emerge, not the angry, irrational Jasmin who had threatened to abandon us.

When Jasmin opened the door, it felt as if the air were sucked out of the room. I held my breath and looked over at Anahita, who also seemed to be holding her breath.

"All of you, start packing. If you don't want me to drive down the mountain by myself, then get ready to go. We will all leave. We're leaving in ten minutes. What are you all staring at me for? Get your stuff together. Now!"

"We can't leave in ten minutes," Mom said, trying to stay calm. "I have to go down to the casino and find Gita to let her know we are leaving. It's going to take me longer than that."

"Gita does not need to know. We are just going to leave. She'll find out eventually." A cruel smile cut across her face.

"I am not leaving without informing Gita and Changiz. How could you even think that we could do such a mean and selfish thing, Jasmin?" Mom asked.

It did not seem possible that Mom, Anahita, and I could do such a mean and selfish thing as leaving Lake Tahoe without telling Gita, but it certainly was possible for Jasmin. She adamantly refused to let Mom tell Gita and kept threatening to just take off if Mom went down to find Gita. She kept devilishly dangling her car keys from her fingers to remind us of who was in charge.

Mom stared in disbelief that her own daughter could do such a cruel thing. She trudged over to her suitcase with her head down and said to Anahita and me, "Get your things together. I cannot allow Jasmin to drive down the mountain by herself. We are leaving with her."

Her voice was an icy mix of surrender and anger. I had never heard her speak like that, and it frightened me. Wordlessly, Anahita had already snapped her suitcase shut. She was on the verge of tears and avoided looking at me or anyone.

I hoped we would run into Changiz or Gita when the elevator doors opened onto the lobby. I looked in every direction for them as we walked over to the registration desk. If we could just tell them we were leaving, then everything would be better—not all the way better, but at least better than just disappearing.

We did not see either of them.

After scanning the casino and lobby, I looked back at the registration desk and saw that Mom, Jasmin, and Anahita had left it and were walking toward the oversize front entrance. Feeling lightheaded and heavyhearted, I followed them out into the moonless night.

Mom sat up front, and Anahita and I climbed into the backseat. As soon as we pulled out onto the road, Mom leaned against her door and closed her eyes. She stayed that way until we got home, either asleep or pretending to be asleep. Anahita and I both stared out our side windows We did not utter a single word the whole way home, which seemed much longer than the drive up. As I gazed out at the piercing stars, I thought of all the things I would do differently when I lived on my own and not with Jasmin. I would go to bed late and wake up when I wanted. I would not boss my roommates around, and if they left their books out or forgot to put the toilet seat down, it would be okay. I would buy American junk food and candy and eat it anytime of day or night, even for breakfast. I would learn to cook Persian food and hold big parties, and I wouldn't get in a bad mood at having to clean up after my friends. I wouldn't be upset if the electricity bill happened to be higher one month or care if I could hear my neighbor's TV through the walls. My house would be anger-free. Period.

I had done typical boyhood pranks before but had never engaged in a bold act of cruelty like this. Even though I'd had nothing to do with the ultimate decision to leave without telling Gita and Changiz and had no power to alter the outcome, I carried the embarrassment of leaving without telling them for the rest of my life.

When we got back to the apartment, I saw that Changiz had left his sleeping bag on the longer couch. I didn't touch it, hoping that when I woke up in the morning, he would be sleeping in it, that they would somehow have found their way back from Lake Tahoe and everything would be better.

Morning came, and the sleeping bag looked deflated with nobody in it.

When Jasmin left to do an errand, Mom took the opportunity to call Gita's husband, who was in Tehran on business. In a voice filled with remorse, she explained that his wife and son had been left alone in a remote town somewhere in the mountains of California near the Nevada border. He told Mom that Gita and Changiz were okay—hurt and confused, but okay. Apparently, they had taken a cab to Lake Tahoe's small airport, and from there they had flown to Sacramento. From Sacramento, they had flown to Minnesota, where Changiz lived. Mom hung up and looked sickly. She sat down at the table and rested her head on her folded arms. Anahita gave her a hug.

"I have a stomachache," Anahita complained.

"Anahita gets a stomachache every time she's stressed out," I said. "Jasmin is like poison. Crazy poison. We can't stand living with her, Mom. If she pulls another stunt like last night's, I'm calling Dad so he can fly Anahita and me back to Tehran."

I said this even though I knew that the situation in Tehran was discouraging. The evening news was filled with images of thousands of angry people marching in the streets, chanting, "Death to the shah."

"You two are better off here in the United States with Jasmin than you would be going back to Iran," Mom said. "I know she can sometimes be unkind and has her outbursts. She is only seventeen years old and does not have much experience taking care of others, let alone her own self. If you go back to Tehran, you may get stuck there forever. No one knows what is going to happen to the country with all these protesters. It could get really bad."

Mom sounded reassuring and convincing, but I had my doubts that Jasmin's behavior was going to change. I decided to put up with her until I was old enough to live on my own.

"I don't want to go on another trip, because I have a stomachache," Anahita said.

"I'm sure it is just your nerves, Anahita. Last night was very upsetting. You'll feel better soon, darling. Let me make you some tea," Mom said.

CHAPTER 8
CLOSE ENCOUNTERS

A couple of days later, Ehsan called and invited us over to have dinner at his place and then go to a movie. It would be my first time going to an American movie theater. I didn't know how much I would understand of the movie, but I was excited to try it.

Shortly after Mom had hung up with Ehsan, the phone rang again. It was Jasmin's immigration lawyer, Pedro Lopez, calling to ask to meet with her today. Since we were already planning on going shopping and the attorney's office was on the way to the mall, we decided to go with her.

I had met Mr. Lopez before and remembered his broad, never-ending smile. He had been recommended to Jasmin because he had a good reputation for helping immigrants change their visa status. When we entered his office this afternoon, his smile evaporated.

Without much of a greeting, he showed us the way to his dark office. He never turned on any lights, and the window shade was pulled down. Anahita and Mom shared a chair, Jasmin took the other chair, and I stood.

"I ... umm ... am not sure where to start," Mr. Lopez stammered. "There is trouble with your visa, Jasmin." He then began to fire questions at Jasmin in staccato succession, as if he were checking them off on the form in front of him.

"Did you enter the United States on a visitor visa in January of 1976?"

"Yes, sir."

"Was the purpose of your visit to see your brother Farhad Alikhani and his wife?"

"Yes, sir."

"Were they living in Stillwater, Oklahoma?"

"Yes, sir."

"Your brother was a student at the time, no?"

"Yes, sir. He was attending Oklahoma State."

"Did you then leave the state of Oklahoma and come to California?"

"Yes, sir."

"Did you inform the INS of your change of address?"

"Yes, sir. When I was in Oklahoma, I applied for a student visa. I also let them know that I was moving to California."

"Did you move to California before the INS in Oklahoma issued you a student visa?"

"Yes, sir."

This time, Jasmin's "Yes, sir" sounded more like an admission of guilt than a confirmation of the facts.

"As I discussed with you before, Jasmin, the INS does not look favorably on people changing states in the middle of applying for a visa. To ensure your student status, you would have either had to wait in Oklahoma to get your visa or gone back to Iran and applied for one there. There are just too many moving pieces in your case. I have done all that I can to obtain a student visa for you, but the INS has ruled against you, and you are to be deported."

The four of us sucked up all the air in the room. I could no longer breathe.

"There is one more thing you could do. You have the option to appeal. Unfortunately, the appeal hearing has been set for one week from today. As your lawyer, I must inform you that that is a bad sign. In my experience, if the INS sets an appeal date so close to the declaration of deportation, your chances of winning are very slim. Your unapproved move to another state while you were in the middle of applying for a student visa is in direct violation of the INS rules.

"I must also warn you that the cost of the appeal is expensive. It is two thousand dollars. I am going to be honest with you: I don't think we would win."

Surprisingly, Jasmin asked about Anahita and me. "But my little brother and sister live with me. I take care of them. They are here legally, on valid student visas. What will happen to them?"

"They should have a guardian. Do you not have other relatives here that can step in as their guardian?" Mr. Lopez asked.

After Mom, Jasmin, and Mr. Lopez discussed Jasmin's situation for a few more minutes, Jasmin agreed to return to Iran with Mom on July 3.

We returned home in shock and dismay. Jasmin was not the nicest person in the world, but she was our sister, and I was used to her. All of a sudden, Jasmin's unreasonable outbursts seemed like nothing at all.

Mom called Ehsan, who assured her that he would support Anahita and me when Jasmin and Mom flew home. That made me feel a little less stressed. If he had not agreed to be our guardian, we too would have had to go back to Tehran, and there was no guarantee that we would ever be able to return to the United States, as a lot of people were trying to flee the unrest, lining up at the embassies in long queues.

That night, a burning pain in my stomach kept me half awake. All night long I replayed the scene at Mr. Lopez's office and woke up over and over again, hearing Jasmin say, "But my little brother and sister live with me. I take care of them. They are here legally, on valid student visas. What will happen to them?"

I did not tell Mom about my stomach pain, as it seemed trivial compared to Jasmin being deported. My stomach pain became the watermark of stress for me, my barometer of emotional well-being for the rest of my life. It was born, like a traveler's parasite, in the United States, as I'd never had the pains in Iran.

The next day the four of us went to Ehsan's home before our planned movie theater outing. We arrived a few minutes before two in the afternoon. Ehsan answered the door in his black-and-white-striped pajamas and hustled us into the living room, as Iran was going to be on the news momentarily. Mahshid served us Persian tea. We settled in their living room, and Ehsan turned on the TV. The first image was shocking. Before, there had been small clusters of protesters shown. Now, there were masses of them. Hundreds of thousands of angry people marched in the streets of Tehran, shouting, "Death to the shah." Burning tires, broken shop windows, and cars on fire filled the screen. We all watched in shock and silence, holding suspended teacups midway between the coffee table and our lips.

At the commercial break, Mom put her teacup down and immediately called Dad. It was twelve hours later for him, so it was the middle of the night. Relief flooded me when Mom said, "Hello." He was home and safe. One good sign.

Dad told Mom that he'd had to close the restaurant early and go home but assured us that the restaurant would be okay because the Iranian army had occupied that particular street and was protecting those businesses from the mob. The street vigilantes didn't seem to discriminate. They were attacking all businesses and shops regardless of who owned them.

"What is happening to our country, Ehsan?" I asked. As I looked around the room, most of the faces reflected back to me what I felt, a sick sense of worry.

"People are fighting for their rights, Borz. The shah has not treated them well."

"What are you talking about?" Jasmin shouted. "Hasn't your family done extremely well under the shah? You have everything you could ever want. How can you defend the people in the streets causing so much destruction and tearing our country apart?"

"Yes, my family is comfortable," Ehsan calmly said. "But that doesn't mean that everything the shah is doing is right. I am not thinking of just me and my family; I am thinking of people who are not as well off as us and how they are treated, what kind of lifestyle they live."

I had witnessed poverty in Iran, but wasn't this the case in every country? I had studied the history of Iran in high school and had been taught that the Pahlavi regime had brought Iran out of the dark ages and into the modern era. The shah's father, Reza Shah, had ousted the Qajar dynasty, which had ruled Iran for 140 years without making any progress or contributions to the wealth or advancement of the country. My teachers had underscored the point that when Reza Shah had seized power, Iran had been a bankrupt country without any signs of modernization. Reza Shah had been determined to turn Iran around. I'd had to memorize the programs he'd put into place, such as constructing an advanced railway system, creating a modern judiciary, and introducing a contemporary education system. The teachers had explained how he'd limited the role of the mullahs, who always opposed modernization, by detaching them from the education and judiciary branches for the first time in Iranian history. Reza Shah had also enforced changes to traditional attire, allowing women to dress as their European counterparts. Reza's son, Mohammad Reza Shah, the current monarch, had continued his father's path and created his own vision to modernize Iran, which we'd also studied in school.

"I am worried that the communists will take over," Mom interjected.

"It will be the end of Iran if the communists take over," Mahshid said. "Did you notice the flags people were waving in the streets? They were mostly flags of communist parties."

"You're right," Ehsan said. "It looks like the communists are backing the mullah."

"Which mullah?" I asked.

Ehsan laughed. "I understand why you are confused, Borz. American news channels show so many mullahs on TV these days. I'm talking about the main mullah, Khomeini. He is the leader of the opposition, of all these people you see in the streets."

"But communists are atheists. Why would they support a mullah, a clergy person?" I asked.

"Anything is possible in a revolution. That's what this is. It is no longer just a group of disgruntled protesters. People are revolting against the shah. When people revolt, it's because they feel desperate and angry and righteous. That combination of feelings fuels them to do rash things."

I could see how angry the people in the streets were, but I did not understand why they destroyed storefronts, came out in thousands to protest, and thought that toppling the shah would solve all their problems. It just did not seem so black and white. Everything was so confusing to me. Everything except one thing: Anahita and I could not go back to Iran. If we returned to Iran, it would be too hard for us to get new visas to return to the United States. We had to stay here.

"Thank you for accepting my request to be Borz and Anahita's guardian, Ehsan," Mom said, changing the subject from vague politics to the concrete problem facing us. "Jasmin and I are flying back to Iran on July 3. My tourist visa will have almost run out, and Jasmin has to leave the country by then. We do not want the twins to return to such unrest, and we want them to continue with their studies."

"Uh, yeah, sure," Ehsan said, with a lot less enthusiasm than Mahshid. My stomach tightened at his less-than-enthusiastic response. I eyed Anahita, who looked relieved. I decided to go with that feeling as well and put Ehsan's hesitancy behind me.

Ehsan, Jasmin, and Mom began to hammer out the details. Anahita and I needed a legal guardian to sign documents and take care of the rent and other bills. Ehsan told Mom that he would visit our property manager and let her know that he would take over the rental agreement as our legal guardian. We weren't sure if we would be allowed to stay in the apartment being minors, but if anyone could work the system to get his way, it was Ehsan. He was savvy at planning, organizing, and being persuasive.

A few minutes later, Nassir and Thuy arrived at the apartment. They were coming to the movies with us that evening. Nassir's natural excited and happy mood preceded him into the apartment with his cheerful hello. They made themselves comfortable in the living room and started telling us funny stories that helped us forget about our immediate worries.

When Mahshid offered everyone ice cream, Thuy said, "Nassir and I were up late the other night, and I got a craving for chocolate chip ice cream. Nassir said he would go get me some. I said it wasn't necessary, but you know Nassir; he always wants to please. So I said okay. It was like two in the morning. There's a twenty-four-hour liquor store a block away, so I expected Nassir to be back in like fifteen minutes. When he was gone for half an hour, I started to get worried. After forty-five minutes, I was pacing the apartment, wondering what I should do. Should I call the cops? Should I go look for him? Had he gotten robbed? I was just about to call the police when Nassir banged on the door. I opened it, and there he was, with bags and bags of groceries! 'What happened, Nassir?' I asked. I was relieved but still worried. 'I decided to get all these groceries while I was there,' he said. I asked, 'Did you get the chocolate chip ice cream?' Nope. He forgot it. But we had milk and cereal and crackers to eat."

We all laughed at the story, which was a typical absentminded-Nassir story.

Nassir started talking about the movie we were all going to see that evening, *Close Encounters of the Third Kind*. From what I had been hearing about it, I was very excited to see it. I had read about UFOs in Farsi and was fascinated with them.

"It's almost eight, and the movie starts at nine, so let's go," Ehsan said, standing up.

When we arrived at the theater, the line to get into the movie was wrapped around the block.

"We will never get in to see the movie," Jasmin complained. "See how long the line is? Why did we come so late? Ehsan, why didn't you plan on getting us here earlier?"

Anahita gave me the big-eyed look she always got when Jasmin was about to have one of her fits.

Without saying a word, Ehsan turned his back on us and fumbled in his jacket pocket. With the flare of a magician, he quickly turned around and flaunted a stack of movie tickets in his hand. Smiling charmingly, he looked directly at Jasmin. "You should trust me by now, Jasmin. I am always prepared. I knew it would sell out, so I came this morning and got the tickets ahead of time."

"Hooray for Ehsan!" Anahita cheered, not only for getting us into the movie but also for stopping Jasmin from ruining the evening with her moodiness.

While we found seats in the theater, Nassir and Thuy bought popcorn and drinks for everyone. With the first crunchy, buttery bite, I realized that American movie popcorn was the best in the world.

Close Encounters of the Third Kind captivated me. Not only was the story compelling, but the believability of it and the special effects seemed so real that they played over and over again in my mind the whole weekend. If all American movies were as good as this one, then I was in the right place for entertainment and looked forward to going to the movies again.

On Monday morning, Ehsan arrived promptly at nine o'clock to meet with the property manager to request that she change the lease from Jasmin's name to his. We all walked Ehsan over to meet Emily Paolo, the elderly, white-haired Italian American woman who managed the units. Her husband, who must have been ten years older than her, was the repairman. When Emily saw us coming up the walkway, she opened her door, smiled, and waved us into her living room. Her apartment smelled of marinara sauce and garlic, with an overlay of strong coffee. Mom, Jasmin, and Anahita squeezed onto the couch, vying for space between the many crocheted throw pillows. Emily sat down on a worn, overstuffed chair and asked us how she could help us.

As Ehsan related the story of why we were there and what we were kindly asking for, Emily teared up.

"Doesn't the INS have anything better to do than mess with such a nice family as yours?" she exclaimed, looking directly at Mom. "Is there nothing that can be done for Jasmin? What about these two dear children? They can't be left alone."

Ehsan assured her that he would check on us and make sure we had everything we needed. Jasmin promised that she would try to come back as soon as possible and said that this was only a temporary arrangement until she could get her papers in order.

Slowly standing up, Emily carefully balanced herself before she went over to a desk buried in disorderly piles of papers. She rifled through the stacks until she found our lease. She then opened a drawer crammed with files, pulled out a copy of a blank rental agreement, and handed it to Ehsan. While Ehsan filled it out, Emily assured Mom that she would look in on Anahita and me and bring over some of her Italian dinners.

Now it was Mom's turn to cry. She got up and hugged Emily. Mom's tears triggered the rest of us, and soon we were all wiping and sniveling. Aware that there were a lot of unknowns for each of us ahead, it was very reassuring that there was one American who cared about Anahita and me. We didn't know how to thank this sweet stranger who, for no other reason than the goodness of her heart, had taken an interest in us.

Back at our apartment, Ehsan called Mahshid to let her know that he had magically managed to get the lease in his name. His triumphant tone misrepresented the fact that he'd had very little to do with it and that it was Emily's kindness and understanding that enabled us to stay in the apartment.

When Ehsan left, Mom and Jasmin began making lists of our relatives in Iran that they needed to get souvenirs for and what souvenirs they intended to buy.

Anahita asked if I wanted to go to the pool. We ran down and threw our towels on a chair, and I jumped in without testing the water with my toes, just as my friend Scott and I did in swim class. When I came to the surface, feeling exhilarated by the cool water, I heard a couple of girls and a boy about my age speaking Turkish in the shallow end of the pool. I went over and started speaking stilted Turkish to them, trying to remember what my best friend back home, Ali, had taught me. He was from the Turkish region of Iran. Those lessons seemed years away.

I could tell by their accents that these kids were Iranian Turks. Turkish immigrants made up the largest minority in Iran, numbering nearly ten million people. Their ancestors had invaded Persia a long time ago, but now they considered Iran their home. Turkish Iranians were not only proud of their history but also proud of being Iranian. They had been known to bravely fight invaders of Iran throughout history.

As Anahita and I got to know these new kids, we saw Mom rushing down the sidewalk toward us. She signaled for us to get out of the pool at once. Walking back to the apartment, she informed us that the high school secretary had called and was talking to Jasmin.

Just as we entered the apartment, still dripping wet from not having enough time to properly dry off, Jasmin hung up the phone. She seemed distressed and said that the principal wanted to see us and our guardian tomorrow. Jasmin called Ehsan immediately. He had just arrived at home and was not happy to have to deal with another crisis for us so soon.

"Ehsan wants to speak with you," Jasmin said as she handed me the receiver.

"How bad were your and Anahita's grades, Borz?" Ehsan demanded, without even saying hello.

"How bad?" I asked. "You must be kidding. I had five As and one A minus. Anahita had five A minuses and one A."

"Are you kidding me?"

"No! I'm not joking," I said, annoyed at the accusation.

"Hmm. That is strange. Maybe they want to give you and Anahita a medal or something. Put Jasmin back on the line."

I handed the phone back to Jasmin. When she hung up, I knew Ehsan was going to have to bail us out again.

Things were moving too fast. Jasmin was leaving with Mom in a couple of weeks. What was happening back home? Was it safe there for Mom and Jasmin and Dad? Anahita and I would be on our own. How would we manage shopping, getting groceries, and cooking on top of going to school and getting our homework done? Now the principal wanted to see us. All these scenarios bobbed up and down in my head as if in a large swimming pool, poking up out of the water and then submerging just below the blurry surface. The images kept me awake all night. What more could possibly go wrong?

CHAPTER 9
UNEXPECTED NEWS

Always punctual, Ehsan knocked on our door at exactly nine the next morning. We all got into his BMW and drove to Andrew Hill High School. The registrar escorted us to the principal's office. Mr. Rogerson stood up and buttoned one button on his suit jacket when we entered. Smiling broadly, he said, "You Middle Easterners like to travel together, don't you?"

"You are right, sir," Ehsan replied. "We like to travel together because we are family oriented, unlike Americans."

Mr. Rogerson's smile faded for a split second and then returned to half-mast of what it had been initially. He sat down at his desk, looked straight at me, and said, "I called you here to give you some great news. You both have graduated from Andrew Hill High School."

He picked up two large manila envelopes from his desk and handed one to Anahita and one to me. I tentatively squeezed the metal clasp together to open the flap. When I pulled out the stiff paper, I realized it was my high school diploma. Anahita and I were speechless.

"How is this possible?" Ehsan asked in his most authoritative voice.

"The achievement gap between these two students and the rest of the school was so high that the administration here and at the district found them to be overqualified for high school. These two kids did exceedingly well in our most difficult classes, including trigonometry, modern algebra, physics, and chemistry, while the kids in their grade level in this school were taking Algebra I. You should be happy about this, Mr. ...?"

"You can call me Ehsan."

"Well, then, Ehsan. I have been in education my whole career and have never had the opportunity—or rather the pleasure—to graduate students so young, students who don't even need to go to twelfth grade."

We thanked Mr. Rogerson and left the school with our diplomas in our hands.

On the way home, Ehsan remarked that the education system in Iran must be far superior to the American education system, since Anahita and I could graduate after taking only one semester of eleventh grade. When Mom suggested we go celebrate our good fortune, Ehsan became silent and speculative.

He told everyone to be quiet so he could think. We all trusted Ehsan to be a problem solver and rode along in silent anticipation. Mom, who was sitting up front with Ehsan, turned to him after a few minutes and asked what was wrong. Ehsan looked a little scared.

"Let's go up to your apartment. We need to discuss the situation, and I don't want anyone to panic."

Just like when you tell someone not to look over their shoulder and they immediately do, when Ehsan said he didn't want us to panic, we all panicked.

"What are you thinking, Ehsan? What is going to happen to Borz and me?" Anahita asked, her voice a little higher pitched than usual.

"We'll talk about it when we get inside," Ehsan said as he parked the car in our carport.

Once inside, Mom, Jasmin, Anahita, and I all turned to Ehsan.

"We have a problem. Since you two are now graduated from Andrew Hill, you are no longer students. That means your student visas are no longer valid. The INS can deport you too."

"This is their problem!" Mom exclaimed. "They never asked our permission to graduate Borz and Anahita, so they'd better fix it."

Ehsan's eyes grew wide. "You are right, Mrs. Alikhani. We have to go back to the school and ask that principal to clean up the mess he's created. I'm calling him right now and will summon *him* to a meeting on short notice this time."

By the time Ehsan got off the phone, he was wearing his familiar triumphant grin. He had arranged for us to meet with Mr. Rogerson tomorrow morning.

That night, I had trouble falling asleep again. At midnight I quietly opened the door to where Mom was sleeping and was surprised to see her sitting up in bed. She couldn't sleep either.

"I'm worried, Mom," I said, sitting down on the edge of the bed.

"Shhh, Borz," Mom whispered. "You'll wake up Jasmin." She grabbed my hand and led me into the living room. "Don't worry, Son. Ehsan always gets his way. He'll fix everything tomorrow. Trust me." She gave me a hug and told me to try to get some sleep and that tomorrow would be a new day.

I went to Anahita's bedroom to see if she was awake. Apparently she could not sleep either. She was sitting up in bed with her nightlight on, reading a book of Persian poems. I looked at her enviously, wishing I had something I could turn to when I felt stressed or afraid. Instead, I only had my thoughts, which raced through my brain as quickly as the scene changes in *Close Encounters of the Third Kind*.

Like clockwork, Ehsan knocked at our door at exactly eight o'clock the next morning. Closing the door behind him, he looked frustrated that my sisters were not lined up with their purses ready to go. He took punctuality very seriously, as he did with every decision he made. Since so much was riding on this meeting, I'd made sure I was ready before he showed up.

"How are you always so punctual and so sure of yourself, Ehsan?" I asked.

"I have learned that it is far better to act deliberately and take control of as much as you can. Being punctual is one of the easiest things to take control of in your life, and it shows you mean business. Be deliberate and be prepared. That way, I succeed in getting what I want. Don't take after your brother, Farhad, who is much more concerned with poetry than the real business of life. Take after me, Borz, and you will do very well."

When we walked into the principal's office half an hour later, we were not greeted with Mr. Rogerson's usually friendly demeanor. He stood up and got straight to the point. "What can I do for you?" he asked.

"Mr. Rogerson, we have a situation here that the school created and needs to clean up. My cousins," Ehsan said, pointing to us with a flourish of his swinging arm, "Borz and Anahita are on F1 student visas. Now that they've graduated, they have lost their student status. Unless they can be readmitted to a school before the end of summer, they will be deported back to Iran. Issuing them diplomas was a dangerous thing to do, Mr. Rogerson. It should not have been done without consulting us first. Their graduation status needs to be undone, and you need to let them back into the school, where they can attend twelfth grade." Ehsan seemed to spit out all those words in one breath. When he finished, he breathed in deeply and sighed loudly.

Mr. Rogerson sank into his desk chair, concern spreading across his brow.

"We cannot take the diplomas back, Ehsan," Mr. Rogerson replied. "They are official government records that cannot be deleted or altered. Now, let me think. There must be some way to get these kids out of this mess."

Mr. Rogerson escorted us out of his cramped office to wait in the lobby. He said he needed a few minutes to think things over.

A few minutes later, we were called back in.

"I feel like we have been put on trial and this is where they are going to say whether we are guilty or innocent," Anahita whispered to me as we entered Mr. Rogerson's small office once again.

I was surprised to see Mr. Rogerson smiling. Anahita and I glanced at each other, and I shrugged.

"Which college would you two like to attend?" Mr. Rogerson asked Anahita and me. "You can go to any community college you want. Even though your GPAs are high, you can't attend a university, because of your language abilities. But you most certainly can attend a community college. Let me know which one you would like to attend, and I will make a personal call to the president of the college, requesting that you are enrolled for the fall term."

"But they require an I-20 form," Ehsan interjected.

"I don't give a damn about the form, sir. Trust me on this." Mr. Rogerson's demeanor had switched from friendly and solicitous to one that mimicked Ehsan's.

Ehsan changed tactics. "We want them to go to San Jose City College."

"Excellent choice! I know the president of that college personally. We were in Vietnam together." He picked up the phone and said, "Shirley, get me Mr. Monroe on the phone."

A couple of minutes later, Mr. Rogerson said, "Hi, Larry. This is Jim. How are you doing?" They chatted about their personal lives for a few minutes, and then Mr. Rogerson finally said, "I have two honor students that I want you to admit to your college. I know it's past the enrollment period for the fall semester, but these two students are in a sticky situation. They are on F1 visas and need to be enrolled in a school. If not, they will most assuredly get deported.

They are excellent students and will be an asset to your college. Can you help them out here?"

Ehsan paced back and forth in the minuscule space between us and the desk as we all waited in silence.

"Excellent! Thank you so much, Jim. You won't be disappointed with these two students … Yes, they are related. In fact, they're twins! … Absolutely. I'll send them over to your office immediately." Mr. Rogerson's cheeriness returned as he thanked the president.

When he hung up the phone, he said to Ehsan, "You need to drive these kids over to San Jose City College right now, to catch the president before lunch."

Ehsan's eyes were filled with admiration. Mr. Rogerson's quick thinking, immediate action, and self-assuredness were the precise characteristics that he himself strove for.

I could not believe that Mr. Rogerson had pulled strings to help my sister and me out. We were basically strangers to him, yet he'd gone out of his way to ensure we would not get deported. Mr. Rogerson would always be someone I respected, and I would think of him for years to come as one of the first Americans, along with Emily Paolo, the property manager, to help me out.

After a round of handshakes and profuse thank-yous, we walked out of the office. The sun greeted us with the same bold brightness as the first day we'd landed in San Francisco.

Ehsan drove quickly to our new school. We hurried up the sidewalk and found the Office of the President. Ehsan announced our arrival to the secretary, who got up and went into the president's office, closing the door behind her. She came out a few minutes later and showed us in. A large, middle-aged man with straight gray hair got up from behind his mahogany desk and came over to shake our hands. He almost crushed my fingers. He actually thanked us for choosing his college and assured us that our applications would get processed in a couple of days. We were to come back the following day with our IDs and filled-out paperwork. The meeting with the president was brief, but we obtained all we needed. We had applications in hand and an appointment with the admissions officer for the following day, and most importantly, we had dodged the bullet of being deported. Anahita skipped down the sidewalk to the parking lot. I ran after her and pulled her hair, enticing her into a race to the car.

CHAPTER 10
FEELING SATIATED

As we got closer to the end of June, the swirly feeling in my stomach returned. Mom and Jasmin were flying back on July 3. The news from Tehran was frightening. A country that most people in the West could not place on a map was now the headline story every evening on the news. I was worried about Mom and Jasmin returning to that mess, and I was worried about Anahita and me being left alone. Beginning July 4, Independence Day, Anahita and I could declare ourselves independent, living in the apartment by ourselves. We were only sixteen and, I felt, too young to live on our own. But we had no choice. I kept reminding myself that Ehsan would be around, and Emily, the property manager, promised to check in on us. That was not much consolation, but it was something.

A few days before their departure, Mom and Jasmin went shopping to buy the remaining presents for our relatives. When they returned hours later, it was already dark outside. Jasmin asked us to help bring in the shopping bags. As I went out to get the last load, she followed me. She told me to sit down in the driver's seat, got in on the passenger side, and handed me the keys. She showed me how to turn the car on and off and ordered me to start her car every Saturday but not drive it until I got my driver's license. It was now my responsibility to keep the battery alive. The next day, she showed me where to sign up for driving lessons when I turned sixteen. All my friends were excited to learn to drive, but the added responsibility of looking after Jasmin's car weighed heavy on me, as it was one more thing I had to be responsible for.

Ehsan called that evening and invited us to Nassir's place for dinner on Friday, June 30, for a farewell party for Mom and Jasmin. I was looking forward to the dinner, as getting together with relatives was a real comfort to me in this foreign land.

On Friday the delectable smells of cooked kebabs wafted out of Nassir's open windows as we approached his house. Ehsan explained that Nassir had made the ground beef kebabs the easy way, by placing them in the oven instead of cooking them over mesquite charcoal, as it is done in Iran. I was excited to try the American kebabs. Thuy was in charge of making the rice. Nassir asked her to make sure the rice was not steamed, as Persian rice is fluffy.

Before dinner, we sat down with tea in front of the television. The demonstrations in Tehran dominated the news. The crowds seemed to have swelled to millions of people on the streets, all of them shouting, "Death to the shah!" Chaos was everywhere. Burning tires blazed. Smoke filled the air. Demonstrators held up their bloodstained hands, shouting that the blood was that of their comrades, friends, and relatives who had been shot by the Iranian military.

"The shah declared a military curfew during the day about a week ago, and I heard it has helped," Ehsan said. "For the last week, the streets have been quieter, so I'm not sure why it has picked up again." Ehsan watched the nightly news and read everything he could on the unrest.

"What the hell?" Ehsan shouted, rising to his feet. "Did they just call the enemy of the shah a holy man? The shah is the friend of the West, not that fool, that mullah! The Western media is betraying us. Those damn turncoats! I know the shah has problems, but nobody with common sense would exchange the shah for that crazy mullah!"

"Why do you think the BBC is supporting the mullah?" I asked Ehsan.

"The BBC, or British Bragging Corporation, as I like to call it, is now taking sides with the mullah because the shah raised the price of oil four times a few years ago. That pissed off the British because it negatively affected their economy. Now they are acting like turncoats by turning their back on the shah and calling him a dictator."

"How do you know all this?" I asked.

"I keep up by reading the British newspapers and magazines! That is what they are reporting. By the way, do you know what triggered these demonstrations and uprisings in the first place? No? I'll tell you. A while back, the state magazine in Tehran ran an article that claimed the shah had accused Khomeini of being an Indian from the state of Punjab in India. This article enraged the clerics, so much so that they went out to the rural areas and drummed up their people to march in the streets. The demonstrations ended up getting larger and larger, until they spilled into Tehran. In Tehran, it snowballed. Anyone who had any grievance with the government or their lot in life or the shah or whatever pain in-the-ass complaint they could think of joined the protesters."

"All this for an article?" Nassir asked.

Ehsan nodded and turned his attention back to the TV.

None of this sat well with me. Questions swirled in my mind. Was what Ehsan said true? Who, exactly, was this mullah, this Khomeini? Was he really Indian, or was that just a ploy by the shah to degrade him? Nobody in Iran cared about race, so the government's claim of Khomeini's Indian origins was probably not meant to degrade him so much as question his passion for Iran. The plot had obviously backfired on the Pahlavi regime, causing the recent disruptions and demonstrations on the streets of the capital. I therefore had to know whether this man was Indian or not. After all, wasn't this one of the reasons people were on the streets, chanting, "Death to the shah"? I filed these questions and many more about the revolution away to be answered when I had time to do my own research. That would have to wait until my current crisis of living on my own with Anahita in a strange country was resolved. I was determined to study the current events on my own and formulate my own opinions.

We all sat down to eat dinner, which was full of enticing, savory scents of Persian spices. I could not remember being so hungry. The kebabs were juicy and scrumptious even though they had been cooked in the oven, but Thuy's rice was almost raw. I filled up on the American-style kebabs.

After dinner, Nassir cranked up the tape deck and blasted the music. We all got up and danced until late into the evening. We laughed and had fun, putting our worries aside. Anahita and Jasmin danced together as if the strife between them had been just an illusion. They beamed at each other like best friends. Mom, in her saffron-colored silk dress, smiled throughout the evening as if this were a typical family party back in Tehran, before Anahita and I had come here, before the country had gone crazy, before she'd discovered she had to escort her oldest daughter back to a fractured city. The couples—Ehsan and Mahshid, and Nassir and Thuy—swayed to the beat, smiling into each other's eyes as the music went on and on. With a satiated and settled stomach, surrounded by those who knew me the best and listening to Persian music, I felt a sense of contentment that I had not felt since landing in America.

CHAPTER 11
NEW FRIENDS

July 3, 1978, was perhaps one of the saddest days of my life. When Ehsan showed up at eight in the morning on the dot to drive Jasmin and Mom to the airport, I was nervously pacing back and forth in the parking lot. I felt a pressure on my chest and had absolutely no appetite. Ehsan parked his Beemer and approached me.

"Borz, why do you look so distraught? You look like a scared cat. Don't worry so much. Mahshid and I will be here for you. Be a man. Be strong. You'll get through this. It's not the worst thing in the world."

His words did not make me feel any better.

Fifteen minutes later, we were on our way to the airport. Mom sat in front, and I sat between my sisters in the back. Small luggage that couldn't fit in the trunk crowded the place where our feet were supposed to go, and more bags filled our laps. The drive from San Jose to San Francisco International Airport felt as if it took four hours, instead of the hour it usually takes. I wanted the time to go slow, so we could remain together for longer, but the long good-bye caused its own pain. Ehsan popped in a tape of Iran's top singer, Dariush, whose songs weave their way into the fabric of our emotions and unite us in the sad anthems of our long history, the invasions by the Arabs, Turks, and Mongols. Dad had said that the Persian culture had been a happy one until we had been conquered over and over again. Now we were all born sad.

Anahita started softly crying as Dariush crooned his popular love ballad. Mom demanded that Ehsan turn the music off.

"Can't you see that the music is making the kids cry?" Mom said. Mom and Dad had never liked Dariush, because he had pushed his political agenda, which was against the shah, through his music. Then he'd gotten arrested by the shah's secret police, SAVAK (or the Organization of Intelligence and National Security). After that he'd turned to singing sad love ballads.

My parents were against Dariush not only because of his shah-slandering songs but also because he was the reason that my brother, Farhad, had been arrested by SAVAK. Farhad had made a name for himself as a lyricist, writing songs for Dariush and other popular musicians. One day, when Farhad was eighteen years old, he and Dariush were walking down the street in Tehran together. An agent from SAVAK grabbed them both, shoved them into a dark-gray Volvo, and sped off. My parents became frantic when Farhad did not show up the next morning. We did not know what had happened to him. We all went to the police station and learned that Farhad had been picked up by SAVAK. My father, usually a mild-mannered man, shouted at the police officer, demanding the immediate release of his son because we had clearance with SAVAK through Dad's catering company, which catered exclusively to the shah and members of his party. The police officer got up from his desk to run a background check on our family.

On the way to the police station, Dad had told us that SAVAK used to be fairly powerless—until it had received trained from the CIA and Mossad, the Israeli intelligence service. My father's voice had caught in his throat. "Anyone captured by SAVAK and accused of being against the shah is tortured."

The officer emerged a few minutes later with an older police officer, and they both apologized profusely. I exhaled audibly, knowing that Farhad would soon be freed. When Farhad returned home later that afternoon, we rejoiced and hugged him as if he had been gone a year, not a day. He assured us that he had not been tortured, although he said the guy who had grabbed him off the street had had the grip of a tiger. Dariush, on the other hand, would be held for a month. I did not even want to know what happened to him during that month. When he'd later appeared on Iranian TV, he'd showed no signs of torture, and the government had allowed him to sing again.

Thinking of Farhad's arrest and release occupied my mind until I looked up and saw that we were turning into the parking garage at the airport. Here we were, about to say good-bye to Mom and Jasmin for who knew how long. God only knew when we would see them again. A stew of sadness and fear sat uneasily in my gut. Once Mom and Jasmin had checked in and were not encumbered by all the luggage, Mom approached me and said, "I'm leaving your sister Anahita in your care. You are now a man. Look after her and yourself. I promise that your dad will be here in a few months with Farhad. I promise you, Borz." Mom was always a strong woman, yet her eyes were a little more moist than usual.

Being sixteen, and now a man, I told myself that I was too old to cry, so my tears went down into my stomach and seasoned the stew of emotions already brewing there.

Anahita, on the other hand, cried freely and loudly. She cried as she did when she was in physical pain. Jasmin started crying too as they hugged each other. Even Ehsan looked sad. When Jasmin hugged me, she told me that she loved me.

"I love you too, Jasmin," I said. "And I'm sorry I wasn't very cooperative these last few months."

"Don't worry, Borz. None of that matters. I will come back soon. I promise."

"You're brave, Jasmin. And strong," I responded. My voice cracked a little. I hoped those that could hear me would think it was just my voice changing and not that I was about to cry.

I meant what I'd said to Jasmin, about her being brave and strong. My sister was returning to a country in chaos, to stand in a mile-long line at the US embassy and try to get another student visa. I had seen the lines on television and did not think that Jasmin had any chance of returning to the United States. Everyone who had the means and was possibly targeted by the radicals wanted to flee Iran now.

When Jasmin and Mom boarded the Iran Air jet, I felt their absence as strongly as I had felt their presence just moments before. They were now gone. Anahita, Ehsan, and I walked empty-handed back to the car. The space in the BMW seemed large without Mom and Jasmin and all their luggage and bags. On the way home, Ehsan played the Bee Gees. The simple, repetitive beat carried us in silence back to San Jose.

As Ehsan walked us up to our apartment, he reminded us that he would take us to register for fall courses at the community college when the time came. He went into the kitchen and opened the refrigerator, which was well stocked. "It doesn't look like you need to worry about food for a week," he said. "Remember, the grocery store is just down the road. You can walk there when you get low on food." It may have been just down the road if you drove, but it was a long half-mile trek by foot.

Then he left. That was it. Now it was just Anahita and me standing in the empty apartment by ourselves.

"What should we do?" I asked Anahita.

"We can go to the pool and then watch TV," Anahita suggested.

That evening, we turned on our favorite television show, *Baretta*. We had started watching it in Iran, where it was very popular, partly because the main actor, Tony Blake, looked Iranian. It also may have been popular because Baretta would do anything he could to catch the criminals, even if it meant going against his superiors. There was something satisfying in watching someone be a rebel for a good cause.

While we were watching *Baretta*, the doorbell rang. I jumped up and looked through the peephole. Emily, the property manager, and her husband were standing there. I opened the door, and they walked in, with Emily carrying a large, covered pot.

"We know your mom and sister left today," she said as she set the pot down on the kitchen counter. "I wrote the date on my calendar so I wouldn't forget. I made you a big pot of spaghetti. It should hold you over for a few days. I hope you like it."

Her husband stood at the front door glancing around the room, as if trying to find something to fix.

"Thank you so much," Anahita said, her eyes shining in gratitude. "Please sit down."

"Not tonight, dear. It's already almost eight o'clock, which is our bedtime. That's what happens when you get old, like us." She chuckled. "I'll pick up the pot the next time I drop off some more food.

"Be sure to lock the door after we leave," she said as she closed the door behind her.

I turned around, and Anahita was already reaching for plates to serve the spaghetti. She took the lid off the pot, and the smell of freshly cooked pasta and homemade marinara sauce spiced with basil leaves filled the kitchen with deliciousness. Anahita scooped each of us a large portion with several meatballs. It was the best spaghetti I had ever had. Once I tasted the first bite, my stomach woke up from inactivity, and I realized that I hadn't eaten all day. I could have finished off the pot, but Anahita put it away, saying we should save some for tomorrow. We went to bed feeling full in one way and empty in another.

Tomorrow was Independence Day, not just for the country but also for us. It would be our first full day all on our own.

I woke up feeling a little older than I'd felt the day before. Yesterday my mother had woken me up, and my older sister had reminded me to bring a jacket with me to the airport, as airports are always cold. Today I had no one to remind me about anything, except Anahita, but that didn't count, because we were the same age.

Anahita asked me why the Americans called July 4 Independence Day. Even though she passed history classes with good grades, she had no intention of memorizing the facts forever. History did not hold her interest. I explained to her what I knew, that the Americans had fought for their independence from the British in the late eighteenth century and then had created the original thirteen states. I told her that I was going to study history in college because I found it fascinating. For me, history was more like putting together a puzzle of the life of the world than merely memorizing names and dates. Anahita, on the other hand, hated learning history but loved creative writing and poetry and was looking forward to studying American literature. Whenever we went to the library, I would check out history books, and Anahita would leave with her arms full of fiction.

While we were discussing what courses we wanted to take, Ehsan called and asked how we'd fared the night before. I told him about Emily bringing us the large pot of spaghetti and said that we had more than enough for one meal.

"You are lucky to have an apartment manager that cooks for you. All mine does is gripe when I park in the guest parking spaces," Ehsan said. "Do you and Anahita want to watch the fireworks with us tonight?"

We thanked him but declined. I told him we were tired today and just wanted to hang around the apartment. Ehsan assured me that he would call back in a few days.

Anahita and I decided to go down to the pool midmorning, when it started to get hot outside. Coming through the gate, I noticed the kid I had seen before who I thought was a Turkish

Iranian. He was with the two girls I had seen with him before, who looked like they could be his sisters. When he saw me put my towel down on one of the plastic lounge chairs, he waved us over. He had a wide, warm smile and unusually large brown eyes in a bony face that gave him the appearance of a frog. The older girl looked a lot like him. She had his same smile. The younger one, who looked about thirteen or fourteen years old, did not smile much at us; she seemed more serious. In English, he asked me if I was Persian. When I said yes, he started talking in Farsi. He sounded just like my friends back home in Tehran, his Farsi having no discernible accent. Therefore I figured he was from northwestern Iran, where they speak Turkish and Farsi.

He introduced himself as Farshid, his older sister as Farah, and his younger sister as Mehri. Mehri had auburn hair and skin as pale as porcelain. Her face was more in proportion than her siblings' were, as she did not have the protruding eyes. We learned that Farshid was seventeen, Farah was almost nineteen, and Mehri was fourteen. Farshid asked us who we lived with. He had seen us with Jasmin but did not know that she had returned to Iran.

"You are living all on your own now?" Farshid asked in astonishment.

"We have a cousin that checks in on us," I explained.

"Does he live in this apartment complex?" Farshid asked.

"No, he lives in Santa Clara."

"Wow! That's rough. Farah can check on you too," he said. "You don't have to feel too alone. There are lots of Persians living in this complex."

I couldn't imagine what coincidence had brought so many Persians to pick the same apartment building in a place like San Jose. I knew that there was a large Persian community in Los Angeles, but I'd thought I was one of very few Persians in the San Jose area. That turned out to be false; there was a burgeoning Persian community right among our neighbors.

"Don't get too friendly with all of them," Farshid warned. "Some of them are communists or antigovernment." I let go an inner sigh of relief, knowing that my new friends were like us and not against the regime.

I asked Farshid what his father did, and he said that his father was a rug merchant who had a large stall in Tehran's Grand Bazaar. At the mention of the Grand Bazaar, a wave of homesickness came over me as I remembered accompanying Mom on many shopping trips there, to get spices, tea, meat, and other necessities. We would take the longer route home, detouring down alleyways where merchants displayed precious metals, copper goods, and handcrafted carpets. It was a sensory experience, with the smells of cinnamon, cumin, and other spices; the deep maroons, blues, and yellows of the rugs; and the shouts and banters of the marketeers. The Grand Bazaar had every kind of business one could need. Dad did his banking there. People came to pray at the mosques. Guesthouses were open for tourists. It was a mosaic of everything that Iran had to offer, with some *hojreh*, or stalls, squatting in postage stamp–size nooks and others ostentatiously occupying two thousand feet of prime real estate. Rug dealers were usually housed in larger *hojreh*, as they needed the space to roll out and display their wares.

Farshid interrupted my reverie when he invited me to play pool in the community room. Smiling, I raced him to the gate, not wanting him to see how happy I was to have a friend who connected me to my culture.

Our sisters stayed at the pool to sunbathe and swim. Right away, I understood how competitive Farshid was, as he was determined to beat me at pool. I won the first game, but he was the champion of the next two games. The whole while, we chatted about cars, classes we'd taken, and people. He loved to draw conclusions by comparing things, like what car was better, who was the most popular Iranian singer, what American TV show was the most exciting. It was his way of compartmentalizing what he knew. Over the next few months, he taught me a lot as he expounded his opinions about anything and everything.

After our third game of pool, we walked back to see what the girls were up to. Farshid asked if we would like to watch the fireworks later that evening with him and his sisters. Anahita and I looked at each other, silently communicating that we had just turned down Ehsan's invitation.

"Yes, we'd love to come!" Anahita blurted, smiling, before I could say anything.

Just before sunset, Farah honked her horn outside our apartment. Anahita and I were excited to go out with our new friends. As I closed the door behind me, I almost shouted, "We'll be back before ten!" before I realized that neither my mom nor Jasmin was there. We could come home whenever we wanted. That felt exhilarating and disconcerting at the same time.

Farshid greeted me by going right into a conversation, as if no time had passed between now and when we had left off talking earlier that afternoon.

"I can't wait until I can drive. When I get my driver's license, I'm going to drive fast, not like Farah. She drives like a grandma!" he said, exasperated.

On the way to the park, I could feel Mehri's eyes on me, but every time I looked over at her, she turned away. There was something mysterious about her that intrigued me. She seemed mature in a quiet way. I was sad to learn that she was returning to Tehran at the end of the summer, as I would have liked to get to know her more.

The following day, the doorbell rang around ten in the morning. I looked through the peephole in the front door and saw Farshid standing outside, holding an empty glass. Unbolting the door, I said, "Good morning! How can I help you?"

"I ran out of milk. Do you have some I can borrow for my cereal?" he asked, strolling into the apartment without waiting for me to invite him in.

As I filled his glass with milk, he asked me, "So what do you want to be when you grow up? I'm going to be a pilot. They get to travel for free, and they make a ton of money."

"I am planning on studying hard and majoring in something that will help me move up the ranks to become an executive or a government official in Iran," I replied. "I'm just not sure yet what that is."

"I just want to be a pilot. All pilots make an excellent income. Why work harder if you can make a good living?" Farshid looked down at the glass of milk in his hand. "I better go before the milk in my glass expires." We both laughed. "Farah is going to pick up your sister around eleven to go to the mall. I'll come over with her, and we can take a walk around the complex so I can show you where all the Iranians live."

When Farshid left, I woke up Anahita. "Anahita, don't buy anything when you go to the mall with the sisters."

"Why not?" she asked.

"We have to be really careful with our money. We don't know when Dad will be able to send us more. And we have to buy groceries, bus fare, books—"

"Stop, Borz. I know! I'm only going to look."

Even though I wasn't feeling the awful pain in my stomach I'd felt right before Mom and Jasmin had left, I still had a gnawing uneasiness, a constant feeling of low anxiety. I was worried about many things, such as our finances, strangers taking advantage of us by charging us too much, having to go to college, and the situation back home. Farshid had said that we were lucky we didn't have an older sister to boss us around. I had not replied, as I kind of wished Jasmin was with us, bossy or not. At least she'd shouldered the responsibility of shopping, making meals, taking care of her car, and much, much more. Now I felt as if it was all on me. Sure, Anahita would take on some of the responsibilities, and she did a lot of the chores around the house, but there was no one older than us. We were it.

My low feelings did not temper Anahita's exuberance to go to the mall with her new friends. She was too excited to even eat the bread, jam, and cheese that I had set out for breakfast.

The doorbell rang, and when I answered the door, Mehri greeted me with "Where's your sister?"

"She'll be out in a minute. Where's your brother?" I replied.

Mehri looked around the apartment to avoid eye contact with me. "He'll come here with Farah when she picks up Anahita and me. I was ready early, so I came over."

That made sense. These three had a way of streamlining everything. The night before, at the fireworks, they'd told us that they all get B plus grades. They didn't study as hard as Anahita and I, because, they'd explained, there was no need. They would skim their reading, understand the gist of it, and move on. I had never thought of trying for mediocre, but it worked for them. They certainly weren't any less happy with the grades they got.

A few minutes later, Farshid rang the doorbell again.

"You're not ready?" he asked.

"Almost. What's the hurry?" I retorted.

"You're slow."

"How? Slow in what way?" I said, feeling defensive, as I was tying my last shoelace.

"Both in moving and in calculating your next move."

I felt somewhat insulted by this remark, but I still admired Farshid. He did move faster than me. It was like he took bigger bites out of life than me. Compared to his, my life was pretty simple. I went to school, studied, hung out with my family, and watched TV. He, on the other hand, already knew how to work on cars. He had taken twelve hours of flying lessons and could copilot a plane. And he was learning to play the guitar. I nicknamed him Jack of All Trades.

Farshid began his tour of the Persians in our apartment complex with unit 23, where, according to Farshid, four antigovernment students lived. We were standing outside unit 23 talking when, all of a sudden, the door opened. A young Persian man came out. He wore a grimace that looked more like his normal facial expression than a response to something. Before he had a chance to close the apartment door, someone from inside yelled out, "Azad, don't forget to buy bread for abgoosht."

"Abgoosht!" Farshid and I exclaimed together. The thought of this Persian soup made of tender lamb, potatoes, onions, and a unique blend of spices caused my mouth to water. I had not tasted it in months. Apparently, Farshid had the same reaction.

"These guys sure know how to take care of themselves here!" Farshid exclaimed. We both laughed.

Farshid led the way to another apartment a few doors down and knocked on the door.

"Do you know who lives here?" I asked.

"Yes. They're my relatives."

A tall, extremely thin guy opened the door. His dark, wavy hair did not detract attention from his prominent nose.

"Borz, this is my relative Nader. Nader, what are you going to do about your nose? It looks bigger every time I see you!"

Nader laughed but told Farshid to shut up. "Please excuse my relative's poor manners, Borz. How old are you, by the way, and how long have you been here?"

I told him that I was sixteen years old and left it at that. I wasn't ready to tell him the rest of my story and figured Farshid would tell him later anyway.

Nader invited us in and made us hot chocolate. While we were discussing Nader's brand-new Grand Prix parked in the carport and sipping on the hot chocolate, Nader's sisters walked into the apartment. They had just come from the pool and were wearing bikinis. Neither of them looked attractive to me. After introductions were made, I felt restless in this strange apartment and asked Farshid to show me the rest of the apartment complex. As we were leaving, the older sister walked me to the front door, saying, "Hey, honey, I'll see you at our party next weekend. I hope you know how to dance." The way she said the last part made me uncomfortable.

Before we made it to the door, Nader shouted out, "Hey, Farshid, have you talked to your family in Tehran? Your father called last night while you were at the fireworks, and he was wondering where you were."

"You don't need to be concerned," Farshid replied. "They are always worried because they have nothing better to do."

Nader admonished Farshid for talking about his family that way.

"Nader is a product of a good family, Borz," Farshid said as we continued down the sidewalk. "His dad, uncles, and grandfathers are all doctors back in Tehran."

I liked Nader for his modesty in not bragging about his good standing in the short time I had been at his place and for his politeness in meeting a stranger like me.

Farshid and I continued our walk around the complex, and he showed me another unit that was occupied by Iranian students. He told me that these guys were into drugs.

"How do you know?" I asked.

"I was visiting them once, and they were smoking weed. One is named Mohammad, and the other is named Ali. Together they are Mohammad Ali!" We both laughed.

"What do they look like?" I asked, wondering if they looked like the famous boxer.

"They both have Afro hairstyles. The lighter one has straight hair but perms it all the time to look like the other one's hair. They kind of bob as they walk, like they're dancing. They both love loud disco music, and there's always a party at their house."

I wondered how Dad could have known that I would run into communists and disco drug addicts when he'd warned me about them back in our home in Tehran. Maybe he had run into these types when he'd been a foreign exchange student at the culinary school in France.

Anahita came home around seven thirty that evening. She was flushed with excitement, chattering about the good time she had had with Farah and Mehri. She hadn't purchased anything but described to me in great detail the clothes the sisters had bought. We both were aware of the fact that we only had $5,000. Even though Mom had come over with $25,000, she had taken most of it back to Tehran with her, as it seemed too risky to leave it in a bank here, where her two teenage children would have access to it.

Anahita told me that they had driven to the mall in Farah's brand-new 1978 red convertible MG Triumph. I had admired that car in the carport but had not known it belonged to Farah. Farshid owned a blue 1978 Ford Cordoba, which was what Farah had used to drive us to watch the fireworks. Farshid wasn't allowed to drive the car until he turned eighteen. He did have his permit, though, and practiced driving on the weekends with Farah.

While walking around the apartment complex, I had shown Farshid Jasmin's 1977 Toyota Corolla. Farshid had made fun of it and asked, "Why on earth would anyone buy a Japanese car?" I hadn't answered, but I knew it had something to do with Ehsan. Japanese cars had not built their reputation at that time, but somehow, Ehsan knew that the Toyota was a good purchase for its reliability. I didn't know why Ehsan and Jasmin had chosen orange for the color, though.

As I thought about cars, the phone rang, and Anahita and I both jumped up to answer it. Anahita got to it first. I could hear Mom's voice through the earpiece. She said that Jasmin and she had arrived safely in Tehran. I grabbed the phone from Anahita and asked Mom if I could talk to Dad or Farhad. She said that Dad wasn't home from the restaurant yet and that Farhad was at his own home with his wife.

"How is Tehran?" I asked.

"The streets have been quiet for the past week. I think it's because they are talking about a new prime minister. The shah has given a lot of leeway to the protesters and the opposition. The current prime minister, Jamshid Amouzegar, will have to step down if that happens. That would be a good thing, as far as I'm concerned. Everything was calm before he took over as prime minister a year ago. Amouzegar jinxed everything. Have you forgotten your Persian history already, Borz? Let me refresh you, but you should remember that before Amouzegar, Amir Abbas Hoveyda was prime minister. Do you remember for how long?"

"For thirteen years," I replied sheepishly. I did not want Mom to think I had forgotten everything.

"Yes, good. That's the longest anyone has ever been prime minister, right? Some prime ministers only lasted a year or even just one month, thanks to the British, who controlled everything and changed prime ministers more often than they changed their underwear. Everything was calm with Prime Minister Hoveyda, though. You must never forget that. Your dad would come home from the restaurant happy that his restaurant was full of customers the whole night. People were content, and the more content people are, the more likely they will go out to dinner. Anyway, Amouzegar claims he's an artist first and an economist second, but he was the shah's envoy to OPEC. You're too young to know or remember what happened when he was the OPEC envoy, so you can ask Ehsan to fill you in on that. He'll know what I'm talking about. I've given you enough of a history lesson over the phone from halfway around the world."

I planned on getting the story from Ehsan, as I didn't believe in jinxes, like my mom did. Ehsan read everything there was to read and listened to all the news reports. Mom gave me one side of the story, but Ehsan seemed to understand all the sides.

"How's Jasmin?" I asked, abruptly changing the subject. Anahita tried to grab the phone from me, but we compromised and held the phone to her right ear and my left ear so we both could hear.

I could hear Mom inhaling her cigarette. "Jasmin is planning on getting her I-20 form from the community college in Indianapolis, Indiana, where her friend Sima and her husband live. Sima is helping Jasmin as much as she can. All we have to do is wait for Jasmin's transcripts to arrive from the schools she has attended here in Tehran. Once they come, we will get them translated into English and then get them notarized."

"What are the chances of Jasmin getting a new visa, Mom?" Anahita asked.

I heard the brief hesitation of another cigarette inhale before she answered. "I'd say it's about fifty-fifty at best, but it's worth trying. One of the problems is that the lines at the US embassy are about a kilometer long now, every day. Nobody really feels safe here anymore. Your dad and I do, so don't worry. Your father is in a good position because he is not involved in politics. But there are many, many people who feel their best option is to leave the country, so they're lining up at the embassies."

"Mom, we made some new Iranian friends," Anahita said excitedly. "They live right in our apartment complex. We met them at the pool. They're really nice. And fun."

"What is their last name?" Mom asked. "I'll look them up here in Tehran."

Anahita quickly told Mom everything about Farshid, Farah, and Mehri, about seeing the fireworks and going shopping with the sisters. She was like a broken pipe; everything flowed nicely until the pipe got a hole, and then it was a geyser of chatter. As she started describing the boring news of what kinds of dresses Mehri and Farah picked out at the mall, I stopped trying to share the phone with her and drifted into the living room. I heard Anahita yell out Jasmin's name, and then the pipe snapped clean in two, and a torrent of tears and gobs of gushes came pouring out of her. I could hear Jasmin also crying loudly on the other end of the line. They missed each other so much, they said. They wished they could be together right now, they said. *Yeah, right. Wait until they really get back together,* I thought. *Jasmin will be bossy and mean again, and Anahita won't say a word. Careful what you wish for.*

When we hung up from speaking to Mom and Jasmin, I called Ehsan. I needed to find out more about "the jinxer" Jamshid Amouzegar, as Mom called him. Ehsan loved history as much as I did and enjoyed discoursing about it more than just studying it. I made myself a cup of tea before placing the call to one of my favorite history teachers.

Ehsan told me that Amouzegar came to power as prime minister on August 7, 1977, when Anahita and I were waiting for our visas to come to the United States. No one knew much about him. He was a quiet economist, politician, and artist, and a long time ago, in 1955, he was appointed the minister of health. Later, he became minister of finance in the cabinet of Amir Abbas Hoveyda, who formed his cabinet after Islamic terrorists assassinated Prime Minister Mansur in 1964. Then in 1974 he became the minister of interior, but his most important role was being the shah's envoy to OPEC. While Amouzegar was in that position, the shah directed him to raise the price of oil four times in 1973. It was a bad move for the shah, Ehsan pointed out, as it created many enemies for him. The worst enemy was the United Kingdom. The UK's struggling economy was set even further back by the arbitrary increases in the price of oil. For that, the Brits wanted revenge on Iran. In some of my earlier readings from the library, I'd learned that the Brits had a real chip on their shoulder about Iran and would always try to seek revenge. The shah was not shortsighted in raising the price of oil, though, Ehsan insisted. He used the influx of money to modernize Iran's infrastructure, army, and agriculture.

He had a vision for the future and was building the groundwork for a modern Iran.

"That was one of the shah's best plans, Borz," Ehsan said. "He wanted to keep up with the times and not have the country fall behind, like some Arab countries."

Ehsan changed the course of the conversation from the past to the present. He filled me in on details I had not seen on the TV news reports.

"Do you know why things have quieted down this week, Borz?"

"No, I don't, but the uprisings seem to come in waves," I replied.

"There's a reason. The protesters are waiting for their leader Khomeini to make a statement from Najaf, Iraq, where he is now stationed after being exiled. Did you see the article in the paper about Khomeini's true last name?"

I had read about that a few days ago. It was baffling to me that publishing the mullah's true last name, Hendizadeh, which means "born in India," would inflame uprisings that were so serious that the government was having a hard time controlling them. I planned on researching this further. It also seemed incomprehensible that the thousands and thousands of protesters would back a mullah. Mullahs were well known among all Westernized Iranians for theft, misconduct, and rape. My family had taught me that they were not people to be trusted.

I wondered if I would have felt differently if I were still in Tehran. Had my perspective changed living abroad? I looked around our simple apartment. It felt like home now. I looked outside at the long expanse of grass lawns. There was a palpable calmness here. That feeling of tranquility gave me security.

Anahita came into the kitchen and relit the kettle. She was smiling and happy. She said she just knew that Jasmin would be back soon, even though Mom said she only had a fifty-fifty chance of getting a visa. Maybe that was why Anahita didn't like history. If she studied history as I did, she wouldn't be able to live in an ignorant bubble of positivity that everything would work out. She could live in her fantasy world that negated facts. I preferred to live in the real world, as uncertain as it might be.

The rest of the summer chugged along in a predictable pattern. I started Jasmin's Toyota every Saturday morning and ran it for five minutes, listening to KFAT 94.5. Anahita and I walked to Safeway to buy groceries twice a week. It was half a mile away, which wasn't far to walk but was challenging in terms of carrying groceries back home. One day, I asked the manager at Safeway if we could borrow one of the carts, but he said that since we didn't have a secure place to put it at the apartment complex, we were not allowed to do that. He suggested we buy a small luggage cart at the San Jose flea market.

The assistant manager, who was standing with the manager, noticed the puzzled look on my face. "Haven't you been to the flea market yet?" he asked as he swiped away his red bangs, which had a propensity to fall across his eyes. He wore a name tag that said, "Hi! I'm Robert! How can I help you?" in bright, bold red letters that kind of matched his hair.

"I don't know what you mean by flea market. I don't want to get fleas."

The redheaded assistant manager laughed. "No, amigo. That's just the name of a place where people go to buy and sell cheap stuff like clothes, stereo systems, tapes, and any kind of junk your heart desires. The San Jose flea market is huge! It might be one of the largest ones in California. But it's only open on the weekends."

"What is an *amigo*, and why do you call me that?" I asked.

"No worries, man. You look Mexican; that's all. You don't sound Mexican, though. You sound like you're from some part of the world I probably have never heard of."

This conversation had diverged to an area I didn't want to go, so I changed the subject. "Where's the ketchup, Robert?"

Robert scowled, pointed down one of the aisles, and mumbled, "Down there. People always ask me stupid questions like that …" He turned and started to walk away, so I couldn't hear what else he was saying.

The store manager chuckled. "Don't worry about Robert. People who don't like him call him 'Ketchup' because of his red hair, red nose, and red face. You must have heard someone call him that."

"I don't know what you are talking about, amigo," I said, turning around to find the ketchup. I sometimes found myself in awkward situations by asking innocent questions that went sideways and got me into trouble.

I grabbed the ketchup and found Anahita in the produce section.

On our way home, we stopped at the Bank of America to check our savings account balance. Anahita stayed outside with all the grocery bags.

When I asked the teller for my balance, she called the bank manager over, probably because of my poor English and strong accent. The manager introduced herself as Mary and asked what nationality I was. I told her I was Iranian. She said she remembered seeing me come in with my two sisters. I told her that my older sister had returned home and that Anahita and I lived alone now. Her jaw fell open. Looking up my account number, she said under her breath that we were awfully young to be living on our own.

"You don't have any problems," she said. "There is $5,218.36 in your account."

"That is barely going to cover our tuition, according to my cousin," I replied.

"Is that the young man that came to open the account with your sister Jasmin?" Mary asked. "He seems like a responsible guy. Is he looking after you?"

"Sort of …"

"Please don't hesitate to ask me for help," Mary said. "I will do what I can to assist you. I'll check your balance every Friday and call you at home if I see money has been wired from Iran. Give me your phone number again. I want to make sure I have it right. I'm so sorry your sister had to leave you two alone."

Outside the bank, I told Anahita that I'd met another American angel, like Emily, our property manager.

"See, Borz? We don't have to worry," Anahita said. "There are angels that help us when we need it. And they are people we would least expect. Everything is going to be okay."

The whole walk home I chewed on what Anahita had said and how she chose to only look at the positive. Yes, the bank manager would call us to let us know what our balance was every Friday. Yes, we now counted on Emily's big pots of pasta every Sunday evening. But there were so many questions we had no answers for. Would Jasmin really come back? And if she couldn't, what would happen to her? Would we have enough money for our college tuition? We were going to college! Could we even keep up in college?

CHAPTER 12
PERSIAN FRIENDS

Four weeks after Anahita and I were living on our own, I called home. As soon as Mom recognized that it was me on the line, she shouted that Jasmin had obtained her I-20 from a college in Indianapolis, Indiana. I wasn't sure where that was, but it didn't sound very close to California. Mom explained that Jasmin's friend Sima, who lived there, had helped her. Mom was going to accompany Jasmin to the American embassy to try to get a student visa for the United States, now that Jasmin had her I-20. Anahita and I were both relieved that Jasmin was getting out of Tehran but felt a mix of sadness and anxiety that she wasn't going to be close to us. We hoped that when she got to the States, she would find a way to come back and live with us without getting in trouble with the INS again.

I told Mom that I was very happy about Jasmin but that the main reason I was calling her was for money, as we soon had to pay tuition. Mom said she would go to the bank tomorrow, but she was uncertain what the outcome would be, as the mob of protesters had burned or broken the windows of a lot of banks. It was hard to hear her over the muffled shouts and mixed noises coming through the phone.

"What is all that noise in the background?" I asked.

"Oh, it's just the demonstrators in the streets again," Mom said, trying to sound nonchalant. Her inhales on her cigarette belied her calm cover.

I thanked her, and we said our good-byes. What would happen if she couldn't get money to us? Would we have to go back? Tehran was now a home I no longer knew.

Ehsan called the next morning, reminding us that open registration at San Jose City College was in two weeks, on August 28. He had yet to visit us since Mom and Jasmin had left, but he did call every other day or so to see how we were doing. I told him I was concerned about money; Mom had said that it was becoming harder to withdraw money from the banks since so many of them were targets of vandalism for the protesters. He tried to reassure us by offering to lend us money until our parents could wire us some, but he would need confirmation that the money was being sent, as he was somewhat concerned about his funds too. His father was a millionaire and sent money all the time, but the situation in Iran was getting worse. People were trying to flee the country and were taking whatever cash reserves they could. The American dollar's value tripling in the last few months compounded the problem. When we'd left Tehran, the exchange rate had been one dollar for seven tomans. Now, with the dollar worth almost twenty-one tomans, it caused many more problems for all of us, and I wondered how my parents could afford for Anahita and me to live here.

Toman was the common name for Iranian currency, although the official name was *rial*. The rial replaced the toman in 1932 at a rate of one toman to ten rials, but shopkeepers, consumers, and just about everyone else used toman when talking about money.

"You really need to watch your spending, Borz. It's tough times, and money is not the easy commodity it once was for any of us," Ehsan reprimanded.

"We don't buy anything but groceries, Ehsan. We haven't spent money on movies or going out with friends or clothes or anything,"

I shot back, a little angrily. "We're trying to be as frugal as we can so we can pay our school tuition."

"Good job. Keep it up, or you will regret it. If you spend recklessly, it will put you in a very uncomfortable position. I'm telling you this because I care about you two and I'm your guardian."

Although he was trying to be reassuring with his advice, it had the opposite effect on me, making me even more worried.

"How much is our tuition going to cost?" I asked.

"It will cost you one hundred twenty dollars each for the basic tuition. Since you are foreign students, you will also have to pay fifty-six dollars per unit, per semester. San Jose City College is on the semester system, which means there are two semesters per year. You both need to take twelve units each to be considered full-time students, which is what you must do to keep up your INS status. And don't forget about books. That will cost you about two hundred dollars each for one semester. Both of you should plan to pay about one thousand dollars each when you register."

I quickly did the math. We would have about $3,000 left. We spent around $500 a month total for both of us on rent, groceries, minor expenses, and other necessities, so the money would last us maybe five months. Mom and Dad had budgeted that we would spend twice that, but Anahita and I were very frugal and did not buy frivolous things.

I thanked Ehsan and asked if he could pick us up at nine in the morning on August 28 so we could register for classes.

He laughed. "If you want to stand in long lines and not get into any of your classes, I'll pick you up at nine. If you want to actually attend college this fall, I'll pick you up at six thirty. Your choice."

"Then can you call us when you wake up, so we'll be ready? We don't have an alarm clock, but I will get one soon."

"I like the way you think, Borz. And how you are watching your money. For being only sixteen years old, you know more than you should."

When I hung up the phone, I told Anahita that we should start buying groceries at the flea market, since I had heard that they were cheaper there. We might be able to get school supplies there too.

The next morning, I called Farshid to see if he and Farah could take me somewhere to buy an alarm clock. He yelled excitedly that he had just passed his driver's license test and now was free to drive me by himself in his Ford Cordoba.

"Let's go to the Eastridge Mall on the east side of San Jose. We can look at lots of pretty Mexican girls."

"Why are there lots of Mexican girls there?" I asked.

"That's where the Mexicans live, dummy. I went there a few days ago with this new Iranian guy I met who just moved into the apartment complex."

"Another Iranian guy?"

"There is more than one. Don't worry; this guy is not a communist. His name is Behrouz, and he comes from a good family. He's way taller than us, like six foot two or something, and skinny, skinnier than you or me. He's also very funny, but his brother is even funnier. Just listening to his brother is a crack-up because his voice sounds like a rooster. You should meet them."

"Not now. I need to buy an alarm clock. Are you willing to help me out or not?"

"You worry like a girl, Borz. We will get the damn alarm clock. By the way, there's a party Friday night at Nader's. His sisters will be there, Behrouz is coming, and I'm going with my sisters. There will be other kids too. You should come. Bring Anahita."

"We have never been to a party here. I hope they don't smoke weed or something," I said, a little shakily.

"Not these people," Farhad laughed. "But the two Iranian guys who are roommates do smoke. Do you remember Mohammad and Ali? Those two are who I am talking about. They aren't invited to our parties and will never be invited. I don't want my sisters around those junkies. And I'm sure you don't want Anahita near them either. They talk like lowlifes and sway like they're dancing some stupid dance when they walk." Farshid's descriptions of people always lightened my mood and made me laugh.

"Why are they like that?" I asked.

"I think they hang out with gangs. Don't worry if we run into them at the pool or in the recreation room. They're okay around guys like us. I just don't want them around my sisters."

Farshid and I went to Eastridge Mall later that day. With his newly minted driver's license in his pocket, he drove as recklessly as possible, going sixty miles an hour in residential areas, screeching to stops, and then gunning the car as if trying to pop a wheelie. Being about five feet two and weighing no more than 120 pounds, he looked more like a twelve-year-old behind the wheel than a licensed driver.

His running commentary on everything and everyone that whizzed by as we flew down the roads had me laughing as if I had not a care in the world. I was sitting beside a comedian who wasn't afraid of anything, someone who stared fear down as he took risks. His attitude toward life gave me courage. I felt as if I too could face the world with courage and laugh at it at the same time when I was around him.

Driving through East San Jose was a new experience for me. There were no white or black people, just Mexicans and Central Americans. Their accents were peculiar, and they wore different styles of clothes. The music coming from the shops was unlike the American music I had been listening to on the radio for the last six months, and the food displayed on the corner kiosks looked completely unfamiliar to me but appealing. I had never been to a part of California that was so unlike what I was now familiar with. Some of the girls even looked Persian, with their dark, deep eyes and thick black hair, and I could see myself dating them. Finding them attractive made me realize that I was free to date whomever

I wanted and did not have to be confined to only going out with my own kind, or Persian girls. Better yet, Mom and Jasmin weren't around to scrutinize who I asked out.

We found a cheap plastic alarm clock with an obnoxious ring that was sure to wake up not only Anahita and me but also our neighbors and headed home. After Farshid screeched into his parking spot at our apartment complex, he introduced me to Behrouz. Behrouz invited us in, and we met his father and younger brother, Reza, who indeed spoke like a rooster with a squawky, unnatural-sounding pitch. Reza and his dad were going back to Tehran in a few days. Behrouz pretended to lament that he would be alone again. He had already lived in the apartment by himself for the last year. He drove a new 1978 Camaro, thanks to his dad being a wealthy merchant, and had a two-bedroom place all to himself at only twenty-one years old. I was awestruck that Behrouz was so independent and capable, until his dad said, "Don't think he's as smart as he seems, Borz. All he knows how to do is spend money. I'm sure you and Farshid know more about math and finance than he does. In fact, when I'm gone, you two could tutor him."

"Thanks, Your Majesty," Behrouz replied, pretending to bow. "I will follow your directions." The lingering sarcasm sliced the silence that followed.

"I just don't want you to get into trouble, Behrouz," his dad said, trying to amend the situation. "Next month, when I come back with Reza, I want to make sure this apartment, the car, and you are still intact."

As we left, Farshid filled me in on some gossip. Apparently, Reza could not get accepted to any college and frequently came to the United States on a tourist visa. He had finally been accepted to Evergreen Valley College, but it had had more to do with his dad's influence or money than Reza's attributes.

"I'm going to Evergreen Valley College too," Farshid announced unexpectedly. "If you took your classes there instead of San Jose

City College, we could spend more time together. I heard that it's easier than San Jose City College. Think about it. Also, why don't you learn to drive? You don't need to wait until your family gets back. You can drive your sister's car now. No one will know. And if you are careful, you won't be caught."

I admired Farshid's go-for-it attitude. He was right. Why wait to learn to drive? I decided that I would learn to drive as soon as possible.

That Friday night, Anahita and I got ready to go to Nader's party. It would be our first party on our own, without our parents, brothers, sisters, or any extended family. Getting ready, Anahita changed her outfit more times than I could count. After each change, she would come out of her bedroom and ask me my opinion, which frustrated her because it was always the same: "You look fine. Can we go now?"

After the fifth time, she yelled, "I wish Jasmin was here. You're no help at all!" She slammed her bedroom door and came back out a couple of minutes later wearing the first outfit she had tried on and shown me.

On the way over to Nader's, we assured ourselves that it was okay to go to the party because we knew most of the people who were invited. We knew that Behrouz and his brother, Reza the Rooster, were coming. Farshid and his two sisters would be there, and of course Nader and his sisters, as they were hosting it. I was pretty sure the communists and drug addicts wouldn't be invited.

Nader opened the door and shyly motioned us in. Reza was already there, popping open cans of Coors.

As we walked in, we heard voices behind us. Farshid was standing on the front step in a bright-pink shirt, black slacks, and shiny black dress shoes.

"You look like a pimp in that pink shirt, Farshid," Nader exclaimed.

"No he doesn't. He looks cool," Nader's younger sister said. "Leave my cousin alone, Nader."

Nader's sister, who had a face that was never going to become pretty, in my opinion, turned around and introduced herself as Haleh to Anahita. Her older sister, who had more of a chance at becoming attractive but was not there yet, shouted over the music that she was Hengameh and that it was nice that we came. Within minutes, they had turned up the stereo and were dancing with Farshid. I could see that he enjoyed being in the middle of two dancing girls, even if they were his cousins.

I glanced over at Anahita, who had taken a seat on one of the dining chairs that had been moved into the living room. She looked completely uninterested in dancing and held that look on her face like a shield to ward off any potential dance partners.

I sat down next to her and asked her if she was okay.

"I'm fine. I just don't feel like dancing. But you should. Go dance with Mehri. I know you like her," she said, suddenly smiling.

I went over to where Mehri, Farshid's little sister, was standing and tapped her on the shoulder. She turned around, and her warm smile melted my feeling of awkwardness. I didn't even have to verbalize the invitation; she took my hand and led me to the center of the living room to dance. She had a way of making me feel as comfortable as if I were with a cousin, not a strange girl. I liked her as a friend, not in the way Anahita had intimated. As we danced, she told me that she was going back to Tehran in the next few days but would return when she was fifteen. I had a feeling she would be back sooner than that, to escape what seemed like the never-ending unrest.

Behrouz showed up with his sister, who had just arrived from Iran the day before. The party was growing. Farshid disappeared for a minute and came back in with a good-looking Iranian guy whose dark curly hair spilled onto his broad forehead. A girl with light curly hair trailed just behind them. They were obviously siblings. Farshid introduced his friend to me.

"Borz, meet Borz. And Borz, meet Borz."

We both were amazed to meet someone with our same name so far from Iran.

Haleh came between us and asked Borz to dance. He obliged, albeit somewhat reluctantly, as he and I were just beginning to get to know each other. Before Haleh had interrupted us, he had told me that his sister's name was Zohreh, which, astoundingly, was Mom's name.

I felt happy and relaxed at this party of Persians, chatting with people with similar names, in my native tongue. School, the protestors, and everything else that worried me stayed far away from me and the party.

CHAPTER 13
DRIVING

Anahita and I left the party around ten thirty that evening and walked home. As I was unlocking the front door, we could hear our phone ringing. Anahita ran in and grabbed it as I struggled to get the key out of the lock.

Mom was on the other line. Before long, Anahita screamed with excitement. "Borz, Jasmin got her F1 visa! She's coming back to America! Not California, but still the same country. She's going to Indianapolis and is arriving in about a week."

Anahita and I were so excited and relieved that we hugged each other, which made Anahita drop the receiver. I quickly grabbed it before she could and told Mom how happy I was that Jasmin was coming back. I said that it was the best news I had heard all year. Anahita was hopping around impatiently, waiting to talk to Jasmin. When I handed her the phone, I knew that it was going to be one of those long conversations my sisters have. Since Jasmin had left, she and Anahita would talk for hours on the phone about girl stuff. They were best friends when they were apart. Anahita and I had had many conversations since Jasmin had left about how much we missed her and all the things she'd done for us. We appreciated her so much more once we had to live on our own and do all the dishes, shopping, and cleaning while also remembering to take the trash out, wash our sheets, lock the doors, turn off the stove, and start her car. Living in this country and this apartment had been so much easier with Jasmin around.

In the morning, I got up and went to start Jasmin's car, as I did every Saturday morning. Behrouz's father was walking by as I unlocked it.

"Nice taxi!" he called out.

"What do you mean? Why do you call my car a taxi?" I asked.

"Don't you remember?" he said, laughing. "Taxis in Tehran are all orange, just like your car. Why did your parents buy you a taxi? Are you going to be a taxi driver when you grow up?"

He walked away chuckling to himself. I sat down in the driver's seat fuming at that foolish man and embarrassed that Jasmin's car was the color of a taxi. Knowing Iranian humor, I dreaded the thought that I would be hearing the same joke from every Iranian in the apartment complex.

I turned the key, and the engine started. Sitting in the driver's seat, listening to the radio, I thought of Farshid encouraging me to drive. Lost in thought and gazing out the rearview mirror, I saw a man with a mustache and dark hair pass behind the car.

"Salaam," he said as he approached my door. "My name is Mehdi. I live in apartment twenty-three with a couple of other guys. Remember me? You and your friend Farshid came by a couple of weeks ago. You met one of my roommates, Azad. I couldn't come out to greet you, because I was in the middle of making abgoosht."

My mouth watered with the visceral memory of the thick lamb-and-chickpea stew. My cautious feelings around anyone who was a self-proclaimed communist or antigovernment protester thawed around Mehdi, who seemed friendly and who reminded me of the savory stew.

I introduced myself. Mehdi told me that he had heard from other folks that my twin sister and I had been living on our own since our older sister had left. He mentioned that he had seen Jasmin around but had not met her, because it seemed to him that she looked down on him, probably because he was a known communist.

"We are not evil, like some may think," Mehdi said. "We just don't like the current regime. And if you believe in democracy, like here in America, then we shouldn't go to jail or get killed over our beliefs. You are probably pro-regime because I have a feeling that your father is somehow connected. You look like you come from a rich family, so it only makes sense. But you're just a kid, and you seem innocent. I doubt you would report me to SAVAK. Even if you did, it probably wouldn't do any good, because SAVAK is in trouble these days. Everyone who is connected to the regime is. It's highly possible that the regime is going to topple soon. Did you know that, young man? If it does, at least I won't have to worry about getting executed if I go back to Iran."

I did not know enough about politics to argue with Mehdi or even to discuss the differences between the protesters' beliefs and the regime's with him. Even though Mehdi's views conflicted with my family's, he seemed like a sincere and honest guy.

"Can we agree to just be friends even though we have opposing views?" he asked, lowering his voice.

"Yeah, I think we can," I replied guardedly.

"Great! Hey, why are you sitting in this car anyway?" he asked.

I explained that my sister had told me to start her car once a week so it wouldn't freeze up. I told him that I wanted to learn to drive but had no one to teach me.

"Don't worry, Borz," Mehdi replied happily. "I will teach you how to drive. My own car is a piece of shit, but I can teach you on this car. Meet me at my apartment at eight tomorrow morning. No one is on the road that early on a Sunday, except for churchgoers, who, by the way, think they are doing themselves a favor by attending church when the truth is there is no God. It's just an illusion.

Religion is an illusion ... Oh, I'm sorry. We aren't supposed to talk about religion or politics." He smiled mischievously.

He reminded me to meet him at eight the next morning and then took off down the sidewalk. As I watched him walk away, I wondered how he could speak so freely about freedom and democracy when the whole uprising was led by a cleric, a religious man—Khomeini. I wondered what communists, who did not believe in a God at all, had in common with clerics and Muslims who were trying to take over the whole country. How could they be allies? I made a mental note to discuss this with Ehsan the next time he called.

Taking Ehsan's lead in punctuality, I knocked on Mehdi's door at exactly eight o'clock the next morning. A man shorter than my five-feet-seven stature opened the door and squinted his beady eyes at me as I stood in the bright morning sunlight. He was at least five inches shorter than I was, with an unfortunate receding hairline for a man as young as he was and a long, dark moustache that looked as if he meticulously took care of it while ignoring the rest of his appearance. He eyed me suspiciously, shading his ratlike eyes with his hand. In a voice a little above a whisper, he introduced himself as Ali and motioned me in with bony fingers. The apartment smelled like abgoosht. It crossed my mind that all these guys did was eat abgoosht and talk about how to overthrow the shah.

Mehdi followed a light-haired guy out of one of the bedrooms. The light-haired guy turned out to be Azad, the guy Farshid and I had seen leaving the apartment a few weeks earlier. He was as unfriendly to me as Ali was. He walked past me into the kitchen without even acknowledging me.

Azad asked Ali what time he'd gotten home. Ali replied, "I got in around six in the morning, just a couple of hours ago."

I was wondering what he could possibly have been doing until after dawn when Mehdi interrupted my thoughts by introducing me to both of his roommates. "Azad and Ali, this is Borz. He lives in unit nineteen with his little sister—"

"Twin. Twin sister," I interrupted.

"Oh, I didn't know you guys were twins. Anyway," Mehdi resumed, "Borz needs to learn to drive, so I'm going to teach him. He has a car but not a license."

Azad looked at me for the first time and laughed. "You are going to learn to drive from the worst driver in the United States. Do you know who this guy is?"

"Yes, he's Mehdi, and he's my new driving instructor."

"No, comrade, he's not just Mehdi, the driving instructor. He's Mehdi, our leader. He is one of the bravest men we know and is willing to die for his country. It's because of men like Mehdi that there is a powerful resistance against the puppet of US imperialism in Iran."

I thought, *Willing to die but living in the United States? That doesn't make sense. Why is he in the States? What did he do in Iran before coming here? What is he doing in the United States to further his communist cause?* Azad's statements reflected the controversial side of our culture for sometimes making claims based on figments of the imagination. I had heard the word *imperialism* before but did not know its true meaning. There was not an equivalent word in Farsi that could be translated to *imperialism*. It was a foreign word, for sure. By "puppet," Azad must have meant the shah. I wondered why they claimed that the shah was subservient to the United States.

I started to feel uncomfortable, almost ganged up on by Azad, who had declared that Mehdi was his leader, and by Ali, who only communicated by way of giving me dirty looks.

"Hey, let's not talk about politics now, guys," Mehdi interjected. "Borz and I agreed to be friends despite our political beliefs."

Azad and Ali left out the front door and took the tension with them. Azad turned to wave good-bye, but Ali left without uttering a word. He flashed me a look that made me feel as if I were an enemy.

I glanced back at Mehdi, who was smiling as if nothing had happened. He grabbed a set of keys from the kitchen table and headed for the door. "Let's go, young man."

I wondered why he called me "young man" as if he were much older than me when he only looked to be about eighteen or nineteen years old. I asked him how old he was, and he said he was twenty-one. I supposed being five years older than me gave him the right to call me young man.

As we walked to where Jasmin's car was parked, Mehdi pointed out an old 1966 Mustang that was pocked with dents of various sizes. "That's my car. I bought it last year for six hundred dollars. The poor thing can barely move. It is desperately crying for attention. Poor baby."

I liked the way Mehdi described his car as if it were a person. He had a good imagination. I just couldn't see why he lived with Ali, who seemed like a robot that just followed orders, and Azad, who reminded me of the Russian Bolsheviks, whom I had just became aware of in my quest to read everything regarding history that summer. Other than its expansive army and ambitious space program, the Union of Soviet Socialist Republics (USSR) seemed to have nothing to brag about from what I could tell.

When we got to my car, I started to hand the keys over to Mehdi.

"No way, young man. I'm not going to teach you by just showing you what to do. You are sitting in the driver's seat, and you are actually going to drive."

Mehdi turned out to be a thorough and meticulous instructor, giving me just enough directions to drive well but not too many instructions to overwhelm me. He had an implicit sense of trust that I was not going to hit any cars, which made me more attentive than ever.

I figured that Azad must have been trying to tease his "leader" when he'd made those derogatory comments about Mehdi's driving.

After circling the parking lot a few times and then tentatively venturing out onto the road, we went back and picked up Anahita.

As polite as Mehdi was around me, treating me with respect and like an equal, albeit a younger equal, he was even more so around Anahita. He always cast his eyes down when he spoke directly to her. He was gentle and peaceful. Later, Anahita described him as an angel. She had never met a man unrelated to us who treated her with such respect. We both agreed that he was not being friendly just to try to woo us to communism; he was just a nice guy who wanted to help us out by teaching me to drive.

Within a week, I was driving on my own. Luckily, my family never asked me about the car when they called. Mom mentioned once that Jasmin was going to buy a new car when she got to Indianapolis, but she never brought up Jasmin's old taxi. My goals were to not let Mom know that I was driving illegally and to not get caught until I could get my driver's license.

One day, I picked up Farshid to go grocery shopping in East San Jose and to buy cheap food and an upgraded stereo for my car. Farshid was fascinated with the lowrider life, and since I had last seen him, he had installed twenty speakers, an amplifier, and an equalizer in his car all by himself. He was brilliant at figuring things out quickly and efficiently. Before leaving for East San Jose, we sat in his car and turned up the radio. I was amazed at the volume and quality of the music that came out of his sound system. The music rocked the car and reverberated off of everything around it.

When he got in my car, he called it a taxi but admitted that he had heard the joke from Behrouz's father.

"I can't wait until that nut of a father goes back to Iran," I grumbled.

"Don't worry about him," Farshid replied. "It looks to me like he retired a wealthy man and spends his time traveling around the world."

"Do you think I can get my car painted? I hate driving around in a car that looks like a taxi."

"Don't do that," he said. "Not having the original paint reduces the car's value. When you get your license, sell this car and get another one. That's what I would do."

As fanatic as Farshid was about cars, he gave solid advice. I couldn't help wondering, though, why Dad and Jasmin had thought it was okay to choose this bright-orange car. Then I remembered that Ehsan had gone car shopping with them. We had been invited to have dinner with Ehsan that evening, so I planned on asking him about his poor choice in car colors.

When I got home, I called Ehsan to confirm that his invitation to dinner was still on for the evening. He asked that we arrive at six and said that Nassir was also coming. That made me very happy, as Nassir was full of energy and always had a way of making me forget about my troubles for a while.

It felt very adultlike for Anahita and me to go to Ehsan's house without Mom or Jasmin. Contrary to being an adult, though, I did not disclose to Ehsan that I was driving without a license. I had Farshid drop us off, knowing Ehsan would take us home later. Anahita and I decided beforehand not to tell Ehsan that I was driving, because we depended on him and did not want to get into trouble with him. It seemed too risky at this point. Ehsan never ventured off the straight-and-narrow path he had carved out for himself and would probably not accept me doing something illegal. We figured it was best to not mention the driving at all.

Ehsan reminded us that Monday was August 28 and that he was going to pick us up to register for school. I was excited and nervous to start college. That familiar feeling of anxiety and anticipation affected my appetite. As much as I wanted to gorge on the sumptuous dinner Mahshid had prepared, I couldn't do so.

Just before Nassir arrived, the TV broadcasted news from Tehran. Reporters denounced the shah as a dictator who tortured the opposition. Frighteningly graphic images of tortured prisoners who had been killed by SAVAK flashed before us. Ehsan pointed out that ABC, CBS, and NBC had all implicitly adopted a new tone toward the shah and that the British were to blame for this new tone. In his straightforward way, Ehsan turned down the volume on the TV and commenced in giving us all a history lesson. He said that in 1973 the shah had raised the price of oil four times. This had hit the US economy hard and had also, among other factors, almost destroyed the British economy. The shah and his decision to raise oil prices was the main force behind both superpowers taking an economic downturn, pushing Britain to the brink of a major recession.

"The British hold a grudge against the shah for this," Ehsan said, "and now they're trying to get their revenge through the press. The BBC is calling Khomeini a holy man, and American press counterparts are mimicking the same message.

"The BBC, or the British Bragging Corporation, is after the shah. I read that the BBC is directly involved with recording and distributing Khomeini's speeches. Listen to him when he drones on: he has a country accent. He's from some small, backwater town. How could someone so stupid have such influence over so many people? I'll tell you how. There are many factors that play a role in this."

Ehsan took a breath to gather his thoughts. He was a very logical person, and I'm sure he wanted to have his mini-lecture come out as precisely as possible.

"First of all," he continued, "like I said, the BBC is helping to spread this low-class mullah's propaganda by playing his speeches on the radio every night. So everyone listening to the BBC is being influenced by Khomeini and is beginning to believe that the shah is evil. Secondly, the shah has many enemies both inside and outside of Iran. But when Khomeini arrived in France, the Western media turned him into some kind of hero. Now this crazy mullah with his crazy ideas is in the spotlight of the Western media. The shah's enemies, Britain included, are giving Khomeini a platform to spread his outdated rhetoric. The more press he gets, the stronger his message, even if the message is foolish and dangerous."

Mahshid interrupted her husband to say that she was turning up the volume on the TV because it looked as if they were reporting on a new development and not just showing graphic photos of tortured captives. I realized that Ehsan's arguments were in line with what Mom had told me over the phone recently.

When the sound came on, the newscaster announced that Jamshid Amouzegar, the prime minister of Iran, had just been replaced by Jafar Sharif-Emami, a man who garnered respect among the religious community.

"This new appointment might be a good thing," Ehsan said once a commercial came on. "Amouzegar has done nothing, absolutely nothing, to calm the situation in Tehran. He just sat in his office, reading the newspaper but not taking any action. I wonder if he only read the comics and not the headlines!" We all laughed.

"He is and always has been a weak man," Ehsan said. "Maybe this new guy, Sharif-Emami, will be more assertive than that pantywaist Amouzegar. Sharif-Emami has an impressive political résumé and speaks his mind. Anyone, though, would be better than Amouzegar. That guy never spoke up even when things were calm."

I recalled what Mom had recently told me about how Amouzegar was a jinxer.

"Now, how does this all tie in?" Ehsan continued. "I'll tell you. Amouzegar took office right after Hoveyda, who was the alleged author of that anonymous news article last January in the *Kayhan* newspaper in Tehran that attacked Ayatollah Ruhollah Khomeini as being a Hindu British agent and a liar. The article inflamed the recent uprisings. Khomeini's supporters called the article balderdash, and it fueled their fight."

Ehsan's cautious optimism put me at ease, and everyone else must have felt that too. There was a palpable smidgen of hope that Sharif-Emami could turn things around. Nassir walked in as we were all chatting excitedly about the new development. His effusive optimism, combined with our nascent feeling of hope, made the evening one of the most enjoyable I had had for a long time.

Monday morning, August 28, Ehsan promptly picked us up at six thirty to register for classes at San Jose City College. I'd had a hard time going to sleep the night before, mulling over one worry after another: money, my homeland, and starting college. On the way to San Jose City College, I used the opportunity to ask Ehsan why he'd chosen the taxi-orange color for Jasmin's car.

"It was your dad who picked the color. Don't you remember that orange is your dad's favorite fruit and his favorite color?"

He was right. Dad loved oranges. Maybe that was why Mom had chosen orange shoes for me in Italy.

Anahita and I each enrolled in four classes to keep out full-time student status active. The only class we had in common was English 1A. Anahita signed up for arts and English classes, and I chose math and physics classes. By the end of the day, we had spent close to $2,000 for the fall semester. When I wrote out the checks and did the math of what would be left in our bank account, the heartburn feeling of anxiety radiated from my abdomen. In the months to come, Mom would try several times to send us money, but every time she went to the bank to withdraw the funds, the government would restrict her from doing so. It became so difficult that many parents, including my own, had to eventually stop supporting their children studying in foreign countries.

As we walked through the campus to learn our way around, we met some Iranian communist students. They were passing out flyers for a screening of the movie *Crimes of the Century Committed by the Shah*. Anahita and I immediately threw the flyers away, but Ehsan kept his, saying he might go to watch the movie alone, without his wife. At first I worried that he might become a communist, but then I realized that he was probably just curious, as he had an insatiable appetite for news and politics.

On the drive home, Ehsan turned on the radio, and we caught the end of a speech by President Jimmy Carter. I had never paid much attention to American politics, but of course Ehsan did.

When President Carter finished speaking, Ehsan turned down the radio and, as always, filled us in on what was going on. "Did you know that President Carter claims to be the human rights leader of the world?" Ehsan asked. He then answered his own question, as he often did. "That's right. His first day of office, he put dictators around the world on notice that the US government wouldn't be dealing with them. This included the shah, of course. Carter doesn't know which way is up when dealing with Islamic cultures. He has some fools for advisers too. At least Nixon had Kissinger. Carter, on the other hand, has surrounded himself with inept idiots. Take Hamilton Jordan, his chief of staff. Why he chose him, no one knows. But Jordan is not nearly as dangerous, in my opinion, as the guy Carter appointed as secretary of state, Cyrus Vance. Have you heard of him? No? You should know that name by now. He has his law degree from Yale, which you would think would help him with negotiating, but he must be too stupid to use it. The shah hates him. Last December, Cyrus Vance visited Iran. Vance may be an idiot, but he did know that when he was placed at the dinner table next to the Iranian foreign affairs minister, and not next to the shah, that he was all but banished. Only the shah makes foreign policy decisions. The Iranian foreign affairs minister has absolutely no power; he is just a figurehead. So Vance left Iran with a chip on his shoulder for being snubbed.

"After that, I read an article where Vance called the situation in Tehran dangerous and needing careful consideration. Yeah, it needs careful consideration, but not the way Vance means. Vance is advising President Carter to cut off ties with the shah. Think about it: the shah has always taken orders from Washington. Now, with Vance taking the wrong side, the situation will go from 'needing careful consideration' to truly being dangerous. I believe that if Carter could think for himself and not listen to his incompetent cabinet, the United States would side more with the shah and actually help squash Khomeini. But not with Vance at the helm of US foreign affairs. And the ugly truth is that the shah can't think for himself. If he could, he would have deported the US and British ambassadors out of Iran for their lack of commitment toward the stability of the region. So we have Vance leading Carter in the wrong direction and the shah flapping in the wind with no support.

"Vance is not acting alone. He's supported by Hamilton Jordan and the vice president, Walter Mondale, who is another fool's choice. The only guy who is standing up to this whole group of clowns is Brzezinski, Carter's national security adviser! Brzezinski is a genius, but no one is listening to him. Instead, Vance and his cronies, Mondale and Jordan, are encouraging Carter to talk to the shah's opposition.

"Here's another of Carter's clowns you need to know about: William Sullivan, the US ambassador to Iran. He is the worst possible ambassador Carter could have chosen. I read up on him. He's known to have lost the countries he's served to local political forces that were not in the best interests of the free world. He was ambassador to Laos in the late sixties, then the Philippines in the early seventies, and now Iran. What did he do for Laos and the Philippines? He lost them to uprisings.

"Anyway, this Sullivan guy lives in Vance's pocket. It's been reported that he is talking to Khomeini instead of trying to help the shah and prevent a revolution. Yes, revolution. Our country, which once was a powerful empire stretching across Afghanistan, Pakistan, Turkey, Iraq, Syria, Jordan, and Greece, is now looking like it will be reduced to a theocracy, a government where religious leaders rule in the name of God."

Ehsan took an audible breath, pausing to let everything sink in. I found myself holding my breath. All I could think was that it was over for Iran. Up until now, everyone had used words like *unrest*, *protests*, and *uprisings*. Escalating the terminology to *revolution* was a whole different game, one in which the Iran that I knew was most likely going to undergo permanent change.

"Khomeini has one clear agenda," Ehsan continued. "It's to overthrow the shah. He is not interested in negotiations. He will not entertain the idea of a coalition government. He wants the shah gone, and that's it. Now he has the West eating the bread crumbs he's tossing out. Carter is betting on this horse and blindly thinks Khomeini is going to turn pro-Western overnight. Nope. Not going to happen. That country bumpkin hates anything that could create a threat to Islamic values.

"Do you know, Borz, what Khomeini's initial opposition against the shah was all about?"

"No, I don't know," I replied. "All I know is that his name and bitter-looking face scare me. Do you know?"

"No, I don't."

"If you don't know," I asked, "how do you expect me to know?"

Ehsan laughed. "I'm just curious if anyone knows."

I realized that if Ehsan didn't know, then no one knew.

"Is there for sure going to be a revolution, Ehsan?" I asked with trepidation.

"Yes, and Khomeini has the backing of the world, starting with the UK, France, Germany, and the United States." Ehsan's voice turned somber. "The shah is finished. The protesters have quadrupled in size and are more violent since Sharif-Emami took office."

No one talked the rest of the way home. Later that evening, Anahita and I discussed in quiet voices that we could now not return to our country. We wondered how our parents were going to be able to send us any more money. Rumors were flying that everyone was running away from Iran and stealing money on their way out. We only had $2,000 left in our bank account after paying the school fees.

I called home and asked Mom to send more money. She assured me that she just had and said that we would soon be receiving $5,000 and that next month she would send $8,000. Those deposits came, as she promised. I did not know at the time that this money would be the last I would ever receive from my parents in Tehran.

One evening, Jasmin called to let us know that she had already applied to the INS for a transfer to Holy Names University in Oakland, California. Holy Names University was a private, co-educational college affiliated with the Roman Catholic Church and run by the Sisters of the Holy Names of Jesus and Mary. It sat chaste and simple in the Oakland Hills.

Anahita was more excited than I was that Jasmin was moving back. As much as I missed her and felt as if I had too much responsibility without her, I had begun to enjoy my independence.

The next evening, I called Ehsan to confess that I had been driving Jasmin's car without a permit. It had gotten to a point where I was tired of parking a few blocks from Ehsan's house and lying that someone had dropped me off.

"For how long?" he shouted in my ear.

"A while," I admitted, slightly embarrassed.

Ehsan was more angry that I had never told him than angry that I had been driving without a license.

"If you want me to be your guardian," Ehsan said, "you have to tell me everything. I get it that you have to drive, and I am okay with you breaking the law about that. If you get caught, you will just get a citation. If you get caught a second time, it could be serious. Go down and get your license. What are you waiting for?

"I'm very angry that you didn't tell me. But here's the deal. If your parents or Jasmin ask me if you've been driving the car, I'm going to tell them the truth. I don't lie." He paused, so that his last words would make a stronger impression on me. "But if they don't ask, I won't tell them. I call it the INS rule. When you get questioned by an INS officer, just answer the questions and give no further information."

"Have you talked to my parents?" I asked. No one had told me that they had conversations.

"Yes, they call every few weeks. I am your guardian, remember. They want to know if you are careful with the money they send you or if you are careless and spend it all. I have assured them that you and Anahita are very careful with your money. In fact, they called last night to ask that I deposit eight thousand dollars into your account. Your father gave my father eight thousand dollars so that I could transfer it to you."

I remembered meeting Ehsan's father a few times in Tehran. He was a very successful merchant with a calm demeanor and always smiled when he spoke. I had heard rumors that he was a loan shark, but my father had dispelled those rumors, saying that people were just jealous of his success as a businessman.

"By the way, my twin sisters are on their way to the United States," Ehsan said. We said our good-byes shortly after that, with me apologizing that I had lied and promising that I would never do that again.

The news of Ehsan's twin sisters, Sara and Soodi, coming to the United States riveted me to the spot in the kitchen where I was standing. Sara and Soodi were a year younger than me and were as unidentical as sisters could be. I had first met them a couple of years ago at my brother's engagement party to Salma, who was Ehsan's sister and who was six years older than the twins. Sara, the quieter, more introverted one, was the most beautiful girl I had ever seen. Her caramel complexion radiated elegance. She'd stared at me with two magnetic eyes that had made me stand still and stay silent. I had not seen her again until Farhad's wedding, but I had been unable to stop thinking about her. At the wedding reception, Anahita had given me an unfurled rose and a note from Sara, which I carried around in my memory as a token of love. In a delicate scrawl, she had written two words: "For you!" Those two words had been the beginning of a trail of love letters that had gone back and forth between us until my parents had sent me to the United States. Sara had promised that she would one day also come here. Now she was on her way.

CHAPTER 14
STARTING SCHOOL

Ehsan knew nothing about Sara and me and our secret love for each other. The only ones that knew were our twins, Anahita and Soodi. And they kept silent about our secret.

Later, I met Farshid at the pool, and we discussed us becoming roommates and letting our sisters live together. That way, Jasmin could temporarily move in with them when she arrived.

When I got home, Anahita said that the bank manager had called and that money had been wired to us from a bank in Santa Clara. I informed Anahita that it was from Ehsan and filled her in on the rest of my conversation with him. When she learned that Sara and Soodi were coming to San Jose, she jumped up and down with excitement, whooping loudly. Soodi was one of her best friends. We were very happy to have our friends, or, in my case, love, coming to the United States soon.

I asked Anahita what she thought about living with Farah, Farshid's older sister. She thought it would work out well since Farah was studious and kept her apartment clean. She was also excited that the younger sister, Mehri, would be moving in with them when she returned to the United States.

I felt as if the ground under my feet was beginning to shift again. Farshid, Behrouz, and I started looking for an apartment in a new complex, as the complex we were in did not have any three-bedroom units. Anahita and I would be separating. School—rather, college—was about to start. Iran was in a state of crisis, and my parents were still there. With all the moving pieces, the one buoy, the one thing I could tie myself to that gave me a sense of stability, was that Sara would soon be here.

The next morning, Jasmin called us from Indianapolis, where she had recently arrived. She was renting a spare room from her childhood friend Sima and her husband, Khosro. Anahita and I remembered when Sima and her sister, Soosan, would spend the night at our house when they and Jasmin were in high school. Their talks late into the night had been punctuated with loud, muffled giggles that could not be contained by the wall that separated our bedrooms. As much as I'd tried to eavesdrop on their conversations through the wall, I had never been able to make out what they were saying. If Jasmin ever caught me listening at her door, she would scream for Mother as if she had been robbed.

Somehow, Jasmin had been able to get her visa, even though the grounds around the US embassy were becoming a refugee camp. Everyone who had the means was trying to flee the country. Most of these people were from the larger cities, as the country folk supported Khomeini and were content waiting for whatever was to happen. American reporters who wanted a different angle on the main story would sometimes venture into rural Iranian and interview the villagers. In rural accents, these uneducated villagers would complain about the general state of things but could not articulate specific problems. They took the opportunity to speak into the microphone to bad-mouth the shah about the poor conditions in villages but made no cohesive comments on what caused it, likely because of their lack of education. I knew that Iran lacked the proper infrastructure in villages and rural areas, but, as I'd learned in my studies of Iranian history in high school, this wasn't caused by negligence of the shah's government. As the shah had said to Western media in many instances, our country had long been exploited by Western powers, more specifically, the British Empire, for its natural resources. The history of Iran's oil industry began in 1901 when William D'Arcy of England secured permission to explore the Iranian oil resources. He discovered oil in 1908 and created the London-based Anglo-Persian Oil Company. The British government gave itself full control of Iranian oil for thirty-seven years. In 1933, the British government forced Reza Shah to sign another sixty-year term and established a flat payment to Iran. They paid four British pounds for every ton of crude oil exported and denied Iran any right to control oil exports. In 1954, a new agreement by the shah enabled Iran to divide profits equally with a multinational consortium that took over the duties of the Anglo-Persian Oil Company. The exploitation of Iranian oil continued until 1973, when the shah signed a new twenty-year concession with the multinational consortium that gave Iran full control of the production, price, and distribution of its oil. In a nutshell, the shah of Iran had five years between 1973 and the 1978 uprisings to build the infrastructure of his country fully. Now an uneducated mullah, Khomeini, was manipulating the villagers to bash the government for the poor living standards in rural areas of the country.

Jasmin promised Anahita that she was doing everything she could to transfer to Holy Names University in Oakland. Sima's sister Soosan lived in Oakland and was working on getting the I-20 for Jasmin. Once Jasmin had the form from the Oakland college, it would take six months for the INS to approve the college transfer. She was not about to do it without approval this time.

Anahita and I shared with Jasmin that we were planning on moving in with friends, that I would move in with Farshid and

Behrouz and Anahita would move in with Farshid's older sister, Farah. Before Jasmin could object, Anahita quickly assured her that our parents had given us permission, as they had already met Farshid and Farah's parents and already thought of them as friends. They had also met Behrouz's parents and were satisfied that both Farshid and Behrouz came from good families.

Jasmin was pleased to hear that our parents had done their research and met the other families, and she therefore supported the move. She would not be back in California for many months, so it made sense for us to live with our friends.

Jasmin did not ask about her car, and I followed Ehsan's advice of not volunteering the information that I was driving it.

As soon as we said our good-byes to Jasmin, I called Farshid and arranged a meeting with him and Behrouz. It was time for the three of us boys to plan our move to a new apartment and for Farah and Anahita to meet and plan their move.

Anahita and I strolled over to Farah and Farshid's apartment that evening. Behrouz was already there when we arrived. He excitedly told us that he had already found a three-bedroom apartment three miles away from where we were currently living. Since Farshid was moving out, Anahita could move into his bedroom with Farah.

The next morning, I called Emily, the kind property manager. As soon as I told her that I was moving, she stammered, "Are you sure you want to move?"

Quickly, I replied that Anahita was going to move in with Farah, staying in the complex.

"I am relieved to hear that. Anahita is such a sweet girl. And you remind me of my grandson in New York. Drop by and see me when you visit your sister."

As excited as I was to move in with my friends and have even more independence, there was a small part of me that knew I was going to miss the invisible Emily. I was going to miss not only her weekly dinners but also having her close by to check up on us. She treated me like family, something I knew Farshid and Behrouz could never do. They were good friends but did not have the kind, loving heart that Emily had.

Emily waived the one-month notice to vacate so that we could actually move in earlier. The three of us went and put down a deposit on the new apartment. It was the end of August, and we were planning to move in Labor Day weekend, right before the first day of school at San Jose City College.

While I was packing up my belongings, I came across a photo album I had put together of my relatives and friends back home and landscape shots of some of my favorite places I had been to in Iran. There was a photo of my best friend, Ali, and me walking up the street to our house. We could have been returning from playing soccer or flying kites. Homesickness hit me hard in the gut when I saw that photo. Ali and I had been best friends. It hurt to know that I now hardly thought of him. Ali had tried to teach me Turkish, and I had shared with him my secrets to mastering kite flying.

I paused at the photos of my family and me at the Caspian Sea. There was Mom, cigarette perched between her fingers, sitting in a beach chair next to Dad and laughing at a joke my dad must have just told her. Mom looked so much younger than when I'd seen her two months ago, when she had visited Jasmin, Anahita, and me and brought me the orange shoes. The photo had been taken just a couple of years earlier, even though now it felt like a lifetime ago. Another photo was just of the sea itself, calm blue water extending past the horizon, with miniature waves lacing the shore.

When Anahita called out for me, I realized I had been lost in thought, gazing at the photo of the sea and remembering the tranquil life I'd had in Tehran, before the words *Khomeini*, *unrest*, and *revolution* had invaded our family and turned everything topsy-turvy.

I peeled off one of the Caspian Sea photos to give to the one person who brought me a modicum of calmness.

Emily opened her front door with the familiar, friendly smile that she always greeted me with and ushered me to her doily-draped couch. I pulled out the photo of the Caspian Sea and handed it to her before she plopped into her favorite chair.

"This is where my family and I used to vacation. It's the Caspian Sea. I would like you to have this photo because you have been so kind to my sister and me," I explained.

"It's a beautiful picture, Borz," Emily said as she gazed at it.

She reached over the table where she had a collection of photos in frames of all sizes and chose one that was obscured by the many photos in front of it. She opened up the back of the frame, replaced the photo with the one I had just handed her, and stood the frame up in front of all the others cluttering the table. "Thank you. I will set it here, where I can see it, so it will always remind me of you and your sister. There is a lot of bad news on the television about Iran. This picture and you two keep it in perspective for me, reminding me that there are many decent people in Iran who just want the same things we do. Stability, education, family."

In a few days, the three of us boys would move in together. I was excited, but the fact that Farshid and I couldn't cook worried me. When I mentioned that to Behrouz, he assured me that he knew how to cook and would make sure to teach us. Behrouz was like an older brother to us. We both felt safe around him. Having to fend for ourselves, both Anahita and I were happy and relieved that we were each going to live with someone older, who could take charge. Farah was intelligent and extremely levelheaded. She comforted Anahita whenever Anahita's feelings started to inch up the scale from apprehension to angst.

"Living with Farah is almost the same as living with Jasmin," Anahita said. "She knows how to do everything, like pay the bills, and she has a car, which will make it easy to shop for groceries. I'm going to miss you, but you're kind of a slob, and I won't miss that. But we'll see each other every day since you are going to take me to school."

Anahita and I both had one class at San Jose City College's sister college, Evergreen Valley College, and three classes at the main campus. When we'd registered for our classes, we had made sure that our schedules matched up so that she could go with me to the two different campuses.

On Labor Day weekend, Behrouz rented a U-Haul for all of us to move our respective things into our new apartment. The first thing we did was load up Anahita's boxes and move them over to Farah's place. When we got there, Farshid had piled his possessions in the living room, so that his bedroom would be available for Anahita. Once the truck was empty, we loaded up Farshid's guitar, boxes of car parts, and other things and took them to the new apartment.

Anahita did not have any furniture to worry about, since we had rented it all. Behrouz had enough furniture for our apartment. I called PG&E and the phone company to turn off the services and the furniture rental company to come and pick up their furniture. Everything went smoothly and was done in a day. I marveled at how easy it had all been and was reminded of the last time I'd moved. Jasmin had gone on and on about how in Iran it took a month to get electricity hooked up after a move and months to get a phone connected. At the time, she had handled all these details. Now that it was me, I understood what she meant. The United States was certainly an efficient country. Not only that, but Ehsan and Mom both appreciated how cheap things were here. Our electricity bill was between eight and twelve dollars a month, and we'd only paid thirty-five dollars a month to rent all the furniture. Now that we didn't have to rent furniture, I could count on saving that money.

Sunday morning, my roommates and I had breakfast together. Behrouz showed me how to boil an egg. He suggested that Farshid and I wash the dishes since he was doing the cooking until we learned how to cook as well. I felt that was a fair trade and didn't mind. Farshid washed dishes a few times but was careless, and I found myself cleaning them before I ate, to get the hardened food off that he'd missed, as well as after.

That afternoon, Ehsan came around to check out my new apartment and my new roommates. After staying a few minutes, he asked me to walk him out to his car. Ehsan said good-bye to Behrouz but did not even acknowledge Farshid. On the way to his car, he said he liked Behrouz but asked who Farshid was. I liked Farshid's put-downs and teasing sense of humor, but Ehsan did not. He found it low class. I told him that Farshid was from a good family and was actually extremely intelligent; he just liked to make fun of people.

"Watch out, Borz. You may find his jokes funny now because they are always about someone else. You may not find them funny when he turns his humor on you."

Walking back to my new apartment, I thought Ehsan should lighten up. He was way too damn serious about everything.

Later, we all decided to explore our new complex. It was like a miniature city with three pools, a Jacuzzi, and a small convenience store. All the units were brand new, and we only paid $425 a month in rent. Split three ways, it wasn't much at all, especially since Behrouz paid a larger share for the master bedroom and a private bathroom. Farshid and I shared the other bathroom. After I saw how sloppy Farshid was with dish washing, I worried about sharing a bathroom with him, but it turned out to not be a problem, as Farshid was hardly ever at home.

Tuesday, September 5, 1978, I woke up at six thirty in the morning feeling wide awake and alert. College started today. Behrouz, who had signed up for only one elective class at Evergreen Valley College, was still asleep. His dad was bankrolling him, so he had no motivation to do anything on his own. Peeking into Farshid's room, I saw that he too was still asleep. I wondered why; I knew he had a full course load, as his father had made it clear that he expected Farshid to graduate college and make his own living.

When I woke Farshid up, he shouted at me to get lost. I was tempted to pour the glass of water that was on his nightstand over his head but did not want to start my day in a fight with Farshid.

I drove to my old apartment complex, and Anahita was on the curb waiting for me. I appreciated her punctuality, especially after leaving my two lazy roommates.

We arrived at City College at eight thirty. We had plenty of time before Anahita's Drama 1 class and my Physics 2A class, which both started at nine, so we went to the cafeteria to get hot cocoa. As soon as we entered the swinging doors of the cramped cafeteria, an Iranian girl with long, dark hair draping over her shoulders approached us, speaking Farsi. She introduced herself as Shahin and thrust a Farsi newspaper, *Shoonzdah Azar*, into each of our hands. *Shoonzdah Azar* means the sixteenth day of the month of Azar in the Persian calendar, the origins of which can be traced back to the eleventh century.

I asked her why the newspaper was called this day of the month.

"You don't know?" Shahin asked, looking surprised. "It's the Iranian National Day for Students. I'm a member of the Confederation of Iranian Students, or CIS, and this is our newspaper." She pronounced CIS like *sis*. "You both should read it. You'll learn something. In fact, you'll probably learn a lot. It's three bucks, which helps us cover the cost of printing it. My comrades and I work all through the night once a month to put it together. You'll learn about the crimes of the corrupt and despicable regime, and hopefully you will soon join us as friends or, better yet, as members."

I looked at Anahita, whose cheeks were flushed angry red. To defuse the situation before Anahita told Shahin off, I took Anahita by her arm and explained to Shahin that we were late for class.

"Don't worry; I'm here every day," Shahin sunnily called out. "I hope one day soon you will read about the crimes of Pahlavi." Pahlavi was the monarchy that the shah belonged to and that had ruled Iran since 1925. Shahin was obviously a student protester.

Holding on to Anahita's arm, I started to lead her out of the cafeteria. I could tell she was still angry from the encounter with the Iranian student.

"How can she be so stupid?" Anahita practically spat out her words. "What would Dad say if he found out that he was paying for us to go to a school with communists and regime haters?"

"Don't you remember, Anahita, that Dad warned us not to get mixed up with communists or disco clubbers? I wonder how he knew that might happen."

"Pahlavi has been so good to our people," Anahita cried.

She was right. Our own dad had had the opportunity to attend four years of culinary school in France thanks to the Pahlavi Foundation. He'd excelled there and, upon his return, had opened the largest restaurant in Tehran. He'd also founded Food Service, a catering company that catered only to the shah's visiting guests and foreign diplomats. He'd received many rewards from the Pahlavi regime. The restaurant was popular, but Food Service was where most of his income came from. SAVAK kept a close eye on Food Service because of its clientele.

Thinking of Dad, I realized that his warning to stay away from communists and disco clubbers without elaborating on why was typical of him. He was a man of few words. He was direct and never expounded on his points. He preferred to get his news from newspapers instead of from the chatty newscasters on TV. When he came home from the restaurant, he chose to relax in his favorite chair by the window and read a book instead of talking about his day or debating the latest breaking news story. Dad, with his thick, dark hair and chiseled Tony Curtis chin, was unequivocally loyal to the shah. His support for the shah was as unbreakable as his loyalty to his own family. He detested communists and mullahs alike. I did not know why, because he had never elaborated, but I assumed it was because they were against the shah.

Hurrying out of the cafeteria, Anahita and I had to pass the CIS table. It was littered with grotesque photos of tortured people. One picture that burned a lasting impression on my brain was of a person so scorched that there were only a few body parts surrounded by gray, lifeless ashes. I could not stomach looking at the photos, but I could see that they had a profound effect on passersby, producing the reaction the "comrades" desired: they were turning people, both Iranians and Americans, against the shah.

As we walked out of the cafeteria, I noticed my former neighbor Mehdi and his roommate Azad.

"Your comrades are busy in the cafeteria showing pictures of tortured people and selling newspapers to raise funds for the so-called revolution," I called out.

Mehdi laughed and said, "They are not my comrades. They are members of CIS, who are not the true fighters."

Azad laughed when Mehdi laughed. "Look, boy," he warned, "don't hang around with those CIS-ies. As their name says, they are sissies, and all they do is party and have fun."

Anahita and I looked at each other, and I knew we were thinking the same thing. If the CIS students weren't radical enough for these two guys, then what party or sect did they belong to?

"Mehdi, what party do you belong to?" I asked. I glanced at my watch; I had only fifteen minutes to listen to his rhetoric before my class. Anahita, not wanting to engage in conversation with an admitted communist, said good-bye and headed off to class.

Mehdi took a deep breath and let out a long exhale of his party's rhetoric. "We belong to the Organization of Iranian People's Fedai Guerrillas. It's the communist organization that's dedicated to the principle of equality for everyone and the dissemination and destruction of the bourgeois ruling class. We oppose imperialism and capitalist monopolies. We consider socialism as the only viable, fair alternative to the greedy capitalist society and believe it is the path to save humanity from war and wanting of too much excess. In our opinion, the full realization of socialism is a global matter. Our organization considers itself a part of the global socialist and workers' movement and relentlessly fights neoliberalism and its aggressions against the standard of living and livelihood of the people, which, by the way, is leading society to decadence and destruction. In other words, my friend, CIS-ies aren't radical enough. They are all about partying and are actually just a gang of opportunists."

Azad laughed. "Maybe you should hang out with them until you become radical enough to join real fighters like us."

Azad, Mehdi's mimic, had teased me one too many times. "If you ever tease me again, I will kick your butt," I warned, stepping toward him without thinking of what it would mean to get in a fight the first day of school.

Before I could swing a punch at Azad's face, Mehdi stepped between us and yelled for us to break it up, pushing Azad away from me. Azad shouted that I was a SAVAK agent. A CIS student came out of the cafeteria when he heard the commotion.

Hearing Azad call me a SAVAK agent, the student yelled back, "Are you out of your fucking mind? How can a kid like this be a SAVAK agent?"

"Yeah, he's only sixteen," Mehdi said. "I taught him how to drive. Leave the kid alone," he ordered Azad, in a surprisingly serious tone.

I thanked Mehdi and the CIS student. I did not really want to get in a fight with Azad, but he had provoked me. I walked to my first class wondering how the opposition to the shah could be so well organized. Those students in the cafeteria were not on campus to study. They were here to dedicate their time to the effort to overthrow the shah. And they had no idea who would replace him. What if the person replacing the shah was worse than the shah?

CHAPTER 15
GIRLS

The month of September brought routine back in my life after a summer of drifting from one thing to another. Every morning I picked up Anahita for class, and we would get our usual hot cocoa in the cafeteria. And every morning we would say no to the comrades who relentlessly tried to recruit us.

At my apartment, Behrouz did most of the cooking, and I did most of the cleanup. Farshid was gone a lot, and when he was home, he rarely participated in the household chores. He wasn't just attending college and studying as I was; he would come home and brag about the many friends he had and the things they were doing. His exploits included cruising around different parts of San Jose, working on cars, playing in a garage band, and meeting girls. His bedroom reflected the disheveled lifestyle he led. On the floor, a dinner plate with scraps of food from a couple of nights ago rested on top of a class quiz, next to a pair of balled-up socks. Somehow, Farshid was able to find anything he wanted in his room. Behrouz, on the other hand, kept his room impeccably clean and tidy. My room was something in between my roommates'. I could not stand to let it get to the state that Farshid's room was in and was equally unable to keep it as clean as Behrouz kept his. In fact, it was just the way I liked it. Over the summer I had grown used to no one ordering me to clean up my room. And it turned out I wasn't a slob, as my sisters had thought.

I called Ehsan in late September to thank him for lending us money until my dad could pay back his father. He informed me that my dad had already taken care of the debt and had already deposited another $7,000 into our account. That meant Anahita and I had more than $10,000 in our savings. Knowing that, I felt the tightness in my chest ease, tightness I hadn't known I'd had until it started to ease. If Mom had left her $25,000 with us and we had this extra $10,000, we could have easily paid cash for a house in South San Jose. There would have been no worries about rent.

Over the phone, our conversation turned to politics, as usual.

"How can so many people support someone as phony and fraudulent as Khomeini?" I asked Ehsan. I truly could not see why anyone would back this angry-looking, uneducated man who butchered the Farsi language with his rural accent and simple word choices. I had grown weary of watching the evening news where it seemed as if every world leader, everyone interviewed on the streets of Tehran, the communists, those on the right, and those on the left supported this maniacal man whose vicious rhetoric against the shah was never questioned or argued.

"The news from Iran isn't encouraging, Borz," Ehsan said. "Sharif-Emami seems to be unable to calm the riots. I spoke with my dad, and he's nervous. That's why he's sending my sisters over here. Unfortunately, I know they won't get along with my wife, Mahshid. They always argued in Tehran. I want you to speak with Anahita about living with my sisters."

"I will talk to her," I replied. "If her current roommate, Farah, doesn't mind living on her own, it would be great. But you would have to help them get a nice apartment."

Ehsan confirmed that getting a nice apartment for his twin sisters with my twin wouldn't be an issue. In fact, he promised to start looking immediately.

"When are they arriving? Do they already have their tickets?" I asked.

"Yes, they are arriving on November 10."

"You have plenty of time to look for an apartment. That is more than a month away," I said while thinking it was *just* a month away that I would be reunited with Sara.

That evening, I called Anahita to tell her that the twins were arriving in forty days. She was excited to see her best friend, Soodi, but did not feel the same about Sara.

"Ehsan is hoping you will live with his sisters," I said. "They don't get along with Mahshid very well. What do you think about moving in with Sara and Soodi?"

"It'd be fun to live with Soodi, but I don't care much for Sara. You know that, Borz, so don't ask me why, because you won't listen to me anyway. I know I brought you her flower that night at Farhad's wedding, but I've always been leery of her. There is something evil about her."

I told her to shut up and hung up the phone. Anahita had said on more than one occasion that Sara always kept her secrets to herself and was tricky. She just didn't know Sara as I did.

While I was talking on the phone, my roommates had come in with three American girls. I was not in the mood to be social and retreated to my room. Farshid knocked on my door and opened it before I had a chance to answer it. I tried to tell him that I wasn't in the mood to socialize.

"Don't ruin the party, Borz. These girls are our age. I met them at Evergreen Valley!"

"They can't be sixteen, like me, unless some crazy high school decided to discharge them because of some idiotic education gap!" I retorted.

"You are acting stupid again. Just get out of your fucking room and hang out with them. It'll be fun. And you'll thank me later."

"I'm not in the mood, Farshid. I think I love this relative of mine. She is my brother's sister-in-law, and she will be here in forty days. I don't want to cheat on her."

Farshid laughed. "Once again, you are acting like a shy little boy. I don't understand why you are so romantic about some relative of yours who's not even here. She must be very pretty."

"Yes, she is. Wait until you see her."

"Sure, but for now just come out of your hiding place and hang out with our friends. They won't bite."

I was in the worst mood possible. My sister deemed that the girl I loved was evil. Now I had to hang out with these strangers.

Ten minutes later, I walked out into the living room. Behrouz was dancing with a brunette girl, and a blonde was entangled in an intimate way with Farshid on the couch. I hated the scene and was about to head back to my room when someone grabbed my shoulder. I turned around and faced a petite blonde girl with big blue eyes. The girl, Katherine, had a sweet, innocent-looking face and quietly asked if I wanted to dance. I agreed but only if the music had a rhythmic beat. We ended up dancing song after song, late into the night, while Farshid and Behrouz disappeared into their rooms with their girls.

"Why don't you like me?" Katherine asked, sensing that I did not want to get intimate with her.

"I do like you, but I think I love another girl."

She said she was impressed with my honesty and asked me to describe the other girl. Katherine was easy to talk to, so I told her everything I could about Sara.

I never saw Katherine again.

CHAPTER 16

THE CELEBRATION OF THE PERSIAN EMPIRE

The shah's seemingly unbreakable and incorruptible dream to build a better, more modern Iran was rapidly coming to an end. I had first become aware of his grand vision for Iran's future in 1971, when I was ten years old.

I, along with everyone else in the country, watched on television the 2,500-year celebration of the Persian Empire at Persepolis, or "City of Persians." Newspapers ran full-page stories on the event, and it was discussed in schools. Persepolis, thirty-eight miles northeast of the city of Shiraz, was the ceremonial capital of the Achaemenid Empire, which was the first Persian empire in Western Asia. The Achaemenid Empire, controlled and led by Cyrus the Great, became the largest empire of its time. Cyrus the Great carved in stone the first version of human rights 2,500 years ago. It amazed me that Jimmy Carter acted as if he coined the term *human rights* in his inaugural address on January 20, 1977. He claimed, "Because we are free, we can never be indifferent to the fate of freedom elsewhere. Our moral sense dictates a clear-cut preference for those societies which share with us an abiding respect for individual human rights." In the end, Carter's support of Khomeini resulted in the deposing of a pro-Western monarch and the placement of a leader who committed some of the worst crimes against humanity.

The shah had a firm conviction that he was part of the lineage of the kings of the Achaemenid Empire. He planned the largest and most extraordinary celebration known in history to honor the monarchy's long lineage and to show the world his agenda of contemporary progress. Planning for the event took a decade. An elaborate tent city was built on 160 acres to host the world leaders. Trees were planted in the desert to emulate what Persepolis looked like 2,500 years ago. The luxury tents were like opulent apartments arranged in a star pattern around a central fountain. Each tent was equipped with telephones and telex connections to the countries of the world leaders. Two hundred fifty red Mercedes Benz limousines shuttled guests to and from the airport.

I watched the satellite broadcast of the event with Mom and my siblings; Dad was at the event overseeing his catering company, which was preparing the desserts for the diplomats. I was thrilled that my dad had a small part in the most glorious event ever to take place in Iran.

In the final day of the celebrations, the shah gave a speech at Cyrus the Great's tomb. The festivities were concluded when the shah visited the grave of his father, Reza Shah Pahlavi. He thanked Cyrus the Great and confirmed that he would continue Cyrus the Great's legacy and grand vision of the Persian empire.

One night in San Jose, a place as far from Shiraz as possible, I asked Ehsan why the US newspapers were now writing about the celebration at Persepolis, an event that had taken place seven years ago. He said that the Western press was trying to bring to light how disconnected the shah was from reality, to show that he did not have a clear understanding of his people and the true nature of the current problems of Iran. Instead of looking internally at what was going on in his country, the shah wanted to use that event to prove to the world how grand Iran was.

"But the whole thing backfired for him with the Gulf States," Ehsan said. "Although the leaders of Saudi Arabia, the United Arab Emirates, and other Gulf States attended the event, they returned to their countries not with the sense of wonder and awe that the shah had tried to instill but with a fear of how powerful their neighbor had become. The entire event played right into their hands, as Arabs always have felt a sense of inferiority and jealousy toward Persians.

"Prince Philip and Princess Anne of the UK, Prime Minister Chaban-Delmas of France, and Vice President Spiro Agnew all dined and danced at the event but came back and made fun of the shah for how much money he'd spent to make himself the center attraction. Now Khomeini has jumped on the bandwagon of criticism and is calling it the Devil's Festival. His words are like sugar pills for the people and the press; they swallow the pills without even asking what's in them. Yes, the festival cost a lot of money. But look at what was built from it. We now have more museums, roads are better, and it employed hundreds of people, including your dad. By the way, the BBC is now calling the shah a dictator. He's a monarch, for goodness' sake!" Ehsan was getting worked up again.

Later, I became aware of what the shah's true legacy was: the White Revolution, so called because there was no bloodshed. The White Revolution included building a modern army and investing in dams and irrigation projects. The shah was responsible for Iran's most robust economy in modern history. He created the literacy corps and a health corps for the large and isolated rural areas. He built relationships with foreign leaders across the globe. Regardless of his achievements, he faced continued political criticism from the clerics, who claimed that his achievements hadn't moved far and fast enough. His character continues to be assassinated by mullahs who believe Westernization is antithetical to Islam.

CHAPTER 17
SARA

One afternoon in the middle of October, Jasmin called with the exciting news that the INS had accepted her application to transfer to a school in California. She had been given permission to move in March 1979, five months away. I was happy but not as happy as Anahita was when I stopped by her apartment to talk to her about it.

One day in early November Ehsan called over at Anahita's while I was visiting her. He let me know that he had found a nice apartment in Campbell for his sisters and Anahita. Campbell was next door to San Jose, with larger, more-expensive homes; good restaurants; and an attractive mall. The apartment was going to be available November 15, which was only thirteen days away. I remained cool about it on the phone, but my heart was sending warm waves of excitement through my body. I would be reunited with my true love in less than two weeks.

"Borz, ask your sister if she is for sure going to move in with my sisters. I need to know if that plan is still on."

I cupped the receiver of the phone and asked Anahita.

"Of course," she replied. "That is the plan. Why would I change it?"

Anahita sounded convincing, but she wouldn't look at me. I wondered why.

When I let Ehsan know that Anahita was still committed to moving in with his sisters, he let out a long, deep sigh, releasing the tension he had been feeling of knowing his wife and sisters might have to live together. They were like oil and water, two substances that never mix well together.

After hanging up the phone, I described Ehsan's reaction to Anahita.

"Of course he was worried. He loves his wife," Anahita said, "and doesn't want any trouble in his home with his sisters staying there. Sara is the cause of it all. Soodi could get along fine with Mahshid, but Sara is an instigator. She gets Soodi worked up about something, and then they blame the problem on Mahshid. I saw it happen all the time back home. I know you don't believe me, Borz, because you have blinders on when it comes to Sara, but mark my words."

I dismissed Anahita's allegations as girl gossip.

One evening, about a week before Sara and Soodi were to arrive, Anahita called me on the phone, interrupting my studying. Before I could even ask how she was, she blurted out that she was not going to move in with Soodi and Sara. I was in shock and could not deal with this devastating news over the phone. I ran out of the apartment to my car and sped over to Anahita's apartment to confront her. Farah greeted me at the door and invited me in. A faint smell of Persian stew lingered around the kitchen. I noticed everything was neatly in its place, a stark difference between my apartment and theirs. I did not remember Farah and Farshid's place being untidy when they'd lived together, but Farshid certainly left a trail of dirty dishes, school papers, and outerwear in our place. He had a way of laughing off Behrouz's and my concerns whenever we brought them up to him. His laugh, his first line of defense, was starting to irritate me.

Farah motioned for me to sit at their dining room table, where Anahita had taken the head seat. They patiently explained to me that it was not fair for Anahita to break her commitment with Farah, as they had just moved in together a few months ago. Anahita did not want to bail on Farah and had decided to stay where she was. She felt bad letting Ehsan down but also felt terrible about leaving Farah. I could see that it was a hard choice for Anahita to make, as she never liked hurting anyone.

Anahita's reasoning was valid, but I did not know how to break the news to Ehsan, except to do it right away in person.

I got in my car and peeled out of the parking lot, speeding to Ehsan's. I drove like a maniac those days, just how Farshid encouraged me to drive. I was one week away from my driving test appointment and felt cocky and confident in my ability to weave in and out of slower traffic. Approaching a yellow light, I laid on the gas pedal to speed through it. Then I heard a siren behind me. A police cruiser signaled for me to pull over. The familiar soup of anxiety bubbled in my belly as I pulled over right across the street from the Winchester Mystery House, a haunted house that the widow of William Winchester, the gun magnate, had owned. She'd had an obsession with the ghosts of folks killed by her late husband's guns. The house's third-floor arched windows seemed to be daring me, the delinquent daredevil driver, to make one false move. The police officer asked me for my driver's license and registration. As I reached into the glove compartment to get the registration, trying to think of an excuse as to why I did not have a driver's license, a compact car flew past us with another police car pursuing it at top speed, lights spinning and siren screaming. The officer at my window yelled at me to start my car and leave, and then he ran back to his patrol car to join the chase. I could not believe my luck. I'm sure I would have gotten arrested for driving without a license if the police chase hadn't distracted my officer and taken him away. I slowly pulled away from the Winchester

Mystery House, deciding to drive more carefully, at least until I got my license the next week. Inching along at the speed limit, I couldn't stop thinking about the coincidence of that speeding car going past me right when I had to produce my nonexistent driver's license. This was a story I would keep to myself. I did not want Ehsan, Anahita, or anyone else discussing the what-if scenarios. They all played in my head anyway.

Ehsan opened the door in his pajamas. He had extricated himself from his living room chair, where he had been studying for his civil engineering test the next day. Books and papers were scattered pell-mell around the chair. He started to spew his usual spiel about how difficult his classes were. I interrupted him to let him know that Anahita would not be moving in with his sisters.

He stood silent for a minute, probably calculating his next move. When he spoke, he said he understood Anahita's decision. Mahshid, on the other hand, did not hide her disappointment. She knew this meant that her sisters-in-law would be staying in their apartment for an indefinite period of time.

Ehsan said that he would be picking up his sisters from the airport by himself, as it could sometimes take a long time for foreign exchange students to clear customs and immigration. Ehsan had obtained the I-20 forms for his sisters. They were to begin classes at Santa Clara High School. They planned on making up the two months of school that they'd missed, September and October, next summer.

Before I left, Mahshid invited Anahita and me over for dinner the day the sisters were arriving. I remembered how nervous I got when I was around Sara back in Tehran. Even though she wasn't coming for a few days, I felt that same nervousness thinking about her now, knowing I would soon see her.

When I got home, I planned on unwinding in my room, as it had been a stressful evening getting pulled over by the police and breaking the news of Anahita to Ehsan. I walked into the living room, and Behrouz called me over. He wanted me to see the newscast he was watching. As usual, the news was about the situation in Iran. Now, though, instead of calling it student protests or uprisings, the broadcasters and journalists were officially calling it a revolution. They were saying that the leader of this "revolution" was a holy man who had come out of exile to overthrow the shah and his dictatorship. Tonight, the media focused on the Cinema Rex fire, a horrifying event that had happened a couple of months ago, on August 19. The theater had been packed, as it had been showing the popular film *Gavaznha* (*The Deer*), starring Behrouz Vossoughi, one of the most famous Iranian actors at the time. Someone had locked the doors from the outside and set the theater ablaze, killing all 422 people inside, including scores of children. Television news stations showed the scorched corpses and burned bodies. The shah's regime blamed the incident on the Islamic militants, while the anti-shah protesters distributed flyers blaming SAVAK, claiming that the shah wanted to make the opposition look bad. Their persuasive powers were high at the time, so most people believed the opposition. Much later, it was disclosed that the Islamic militants had set the fire to discredit the regime.

During a much-needed commercial break, Behrouz described the photos of people tortured by SAVAK that were now peppering the news on ABC and NBC. Now I no longer needed to go to anti-regime seminars and gatherings; the Western press was doing a bang-up job turning the shah from a modern, pro-Western monarch into the greatest enemy of human rights practically overnight.

Behrouz was indifferent to politics and was ignorant of history. He did not believe in any system, because he did not have the background knowledge to form educated opinions. His underlying belief was that the shah had made some mistakes and was now paying for it. He, like many students here and back in Iran, did not think about what the consequences would be if the shah was overthrown. The pinnacle question that no one wanted to look at was, who would replace the shah? The tide of opinion had swung so that practically everyone wanted the shah to go and were willing to pay the unknown price.

Ehsan called to tell me to watch the news. I told him that I was already watching it and asked him who would take the shah's place if the opposition was successful in toppling him.

"It's not clear what this mullah wants except for the shah to leave Iran," Ehsan said. "He's now in Paris living in a house paid for by the French government because Saddam Hussein wanted to deport him. In fact, I heard on the BBC that Saddam offered to have this asshole arrested when he was in Iraq, but the shah refused. What an incomprehensible mistake the shah made, not having Khomeini arrested. This mullah is now in the spotlight of the Western press, and he's turning every incident against the shah, like the incident at the Rex theater."

It seemed that whatever the shah did those days to change the situation in Iran only made things worse.

When the news programs were over, Behrouz and I flipped off the TV and turned on the radio. The song "Sometimes When We Touch" by Dan Hill came on. That song is one of the saddest and most touching songs I have ever heard. It seemed appropriate to listen to it now, as my country was breaking apart.

November 10 was a memorable day, one that still steals my breath when I pause to remember the events. It was an uncommonly dark Saturday morning. The fog was lathered so thick on the earth that it reduced visibility to a few feet in front of me. The darkness felt like sadness, as if the world were crying about something. Maybe it was crying about the troubles back home and the tortured bodies that were now not only displayed on television screens but also parading in black and white in my head as I slept, tormenting me in my dreams. The fogginess seemed incompatible with the impending arrival of Sara and Soodi.

Ehsan called that morning to remind me that he was going to the airport to pick up his sisters and that we were invited over for dinner that evening. I could hear a strain behind his voice; he knew that he was delivering disharmony to his apartment by picking up his sisters.

Ehsan was in a tough spot. His sisters were too young to live on their own, and rooming with Anahita, who, by the way, was not much older than them, was now not an option. Ehsan and Mahshid would have to make room in their home for the twins. And if it did not work out, Ehsan would have to call his dad to send his sisters back. That was what he'd told me when I had informed him that Anahita was not going to move in with Soodi and Sara.

I did not like to think of that possibility. I had waited a long time to see Sara again and could not imagine her returning to Iran so soon.

Ehsan was a mentor to me. He was the only adult in my life who actively guided me and looked after me. I felt that Anahita and I had been left alone to look after ourselves in a foreign country. It bothered me that Mom and Dad rarely called us. We would call them periodically. Since it was so expensive to place a call to Tehran, we would just exchange a few words with them before asking for money. They would reply that they would send money as soon as they could. I used to look forward to talking to Mom after school, on the days she was home. Now I just had my roommates to come home to, who didn't really care about what I'd learned or what I'd done.

I sometimes wondered if my parents cared about us at all. They did not know what I did on a daily basis. They did not know what I ate or if I showered or did my homework. They really did not know anything about me.

And I did not know about their motives. Why had it been so important that they send us here to go to school?

They must have cared about us, as they were paying for us to live here, but they both were masters at minimizing problems. They downplayed the turmoil they must have been experiencing in Tehran. Maybe they'd sent us, their teenage children, out of the country to protect us from the uprisings. If that was true and if they really did care that much about us and our safety, how could they stay so distant from knowing what went on with us every day? They did not know how wearying it was to worry about paying bills and purchasing groceries and school supplies and how exhausting it was to avoid the comrades and other communists on campus. I tended to dwell on worst-case scenarios, which only added to my growing inbox of worries. Lying in bed at night, I wondered how Mom could sleep not knowing exactly where I was at that very moment. Did she stay up worrying about us as I did wondering and worrying about them?

I focused my anger and disappointment on Mom because Dad had never been around much. He had always been out checking up on his restaurant, working at the catering company, or stopping by the Pahlavi Foundation to collect his checks for catering royal events. He had never paid much attention to my siblings and me.

Neither parent had ever helped me with homework. Fortunately, both Anahita and I must have been born with a good work ethic, and we both valued getting things done, whether it was writing an essay or making sure the laundry was washed and folded before the week began. Looking back, I think this ethic helped us survive on our own at such a young age.

I tended to try to solve people problems like math problems. People reacted or did things for a reason. If I knew the reason, or variable, then I could understand, or solve, that person. I just couldn't figure out the reason for Mom not to be worried about Anahita and me, thousands of miles away and now not even living together.

Mom was home in the afternoons on the days she wasn't helping out my aunt. Her sister had seven daughters and one son. She was married to an unsuccessful wood merchant who struggled to support his eight children. Mom was like a second mother to her nieces and nephews and spent most days helping her sister care for them. She treated her time spent there like a job, a place where she was needed and appreciated. It gave her a sense of purpose.

Mom was a talented artist but had not been given the opportunity to pursue art. In her day, parents seldom sent their daughters overseas to get an education. Girls were forced to marry young. When Mom was sixteen years old, she married the first man who asked her parents for her hand. That young man was my father, her handsome twenty-five-year-old first cousin. Their mothers were sisters. As was customary, cousins married each other to keep the wealth in the family. My family had made a tentative arrangement for me to marry my first cousin Narges when I returned from the United States. I had overheard my parents and her parents talking about it when I was twelve years old.

Mom became an adult on her wedding day. Before her wedding, she was a typical teenager, involved with her friends, dependent on her parents, and unaware of what being a responsible adult meant. She and Dad had to figure out how to live in an apartment together, pay bills, do chores, and make meals on their own. The biggest challenge they faced was parenting. Getting married as a teenager did not give my mom any experience in raising teenagers. I realized that Mom married at about the same age I was right now. Regardless, I churned and chewed on why it seemed so careless to me for her and Dad to send Anahita and me halfway across the world to live with our seventeen-year-old sister, Jasmin.

The night of Sara and Soodi's arrival, I picked up Anahita and drove to Ehsan's house. When Mahshid opened the door, ghormeh sabzi, a popular Persian herb stew, wafted out the door and into my nose, trying to awake my appetite. However, the knowledge I was about to come face-to-face with Sara clamped my stomach shut like a vault. I felt a little faint, which could have been from breathing so shallowly.

Mahshid returned to the kitchen to tend to the dinner preparations. Ehsan was out picking up some soda at the nearby grocery store. Anahita promptly ran into the bedroom where the twins were, and I immediately heard the three of them squealing and laughing. Standing alone in the living room, I did not know whether I should follow Anahita or take a seat. Then Sara walked out of the bedroom.

She was more beautiful than I remembered. Her olive skin was flawless. Loopy, soft curls framed her heart-shaped face like a movie star's. As she walked toward me, she looked straight at me, or through me, or into me, with her deep, dark eyes. I could not breathe.

"How are you doing, Borz?" she asked, almost nonchalantly. "Long time no see. You forgot all about me when you landed here and started dating those beautiful blondes."

I composed myself enough to emit a sound between a scoff and a laugh and replied, "The last time one of them came close to me, I told her to get lost."

We locked our gazes on each other. Time stopped. I could practically hear my heart thumping in my chest.

"Why?" she asked after several moments.

"You know why," I answered.

I broke off our gaze and ran outside to the backyard, gulping air. I could not breathe when Sara was around. It was like she had a kind of spell over me. The only way I could rationalize that spell was to identify it as love. I was more in love with Sara now than ever before.

Sara stood at the door watching me. Her gaze was enchanting. When she disappeared from the doorway, I followed her back into the house. We resumed our stance in the living room, my eyes locked with hers.

The front door of the apartment slammed, and we heard the crackling of the paper bags Ehsan was carrying. He came into the living room and asked, "Why are you two staring at each other?"

Not only was my voice not within my command, but I also did not know how to answer that question.

Sara had an answer ready. "Borz just walked in, and we didn't recognize each other."

Ehsan left the room, lugging the paper bags of sodas to the kitchen. Sara and I both sighed deep exhales of relief, knowing that our secret love was still a secret.

Mahshid called us to the table for dinner. Anahita chatted with Soodi practically nonstop through dinner. At least her chatter was a distraction for me. Although the stew smelled sumptuous, I could not stomach much of it. Mahshid asked if I was not well, as she'd noticed that I was twirling my spoon in my bowl without actually taking any bites. I told her that I felt a little ill.

"You worry too much, Borz," Mahshid scolded. "You have ever since I first met you. Try to relax a bit. Soodi and Sara have just arrived. Put on a good face for them."

If only you knew how aware I am that Sara is in the same room as me, I thought.

The next morning, after a sleepless night, I informed Farshid that Sara had arrived. He laughed it off, like it was no big deal. When Behrouz came into the kitchen, Farshid announced, "The one and only beautiful girlfriend of Borz has graced San Jose with her presence."

Behrouz, who is usually sleepy and nontalkative first thing in the morning, perked up. "You have a girlfriend, Borz?" he asked. "Tell me, what's it like being in love?"

"It sucks!" I grumbled. "You can't stop thinking about the girl you love. Being in love takes over your whole brain."

"What's wrong with that?"

"Wait and see."

As much as I loved Sara and was overjoyed that she was here, I felt troubled. I had enough instability in my life being here, and this was one more variable, one more thing I had to solve. Maybe I was too young to be in love, or at least too young to not be troubled by being in love. We were too young to marry. I couldn't take care of her. I didn't know how to be a boyfriend. All I knew was that there was an unbreakable and incorruptible bond between us.

A week later, Farshid burst into the living room to brag about the ticket he'd gotten while going 120 miles an hour across the Bay Bridge. He strutted around like a rooster, with his chest puffed up and head bobbing.

"What was the cop's reaction, Farshid?" asked Behrouz, who was enjoying the story.

"There were a couple of cops, but they didn't take me to the station, of course," Farshid replied with a look-who-they-were-dealing-with attitude.

"Maybe they let you go because they felt sorry for you since you are only about five feet tall and barely weigh a hundred pounds," Behrouz teased. "They didn't want to arrest a child!"

Farshid looked as if he wanted to punch Behrouz, but Farshid was scared of this tall Iranian and would never do it. Farshid only picked on people his own size. I had wrestled Behrouz a couple of times and knew he was a gentle giant. He put no force behind his swings. He just was not a fighter.

"Maybe you should quit karate and put on some weight," Behrouz continued. "I'm sure the cops would arrest you if you looked like a man. Then you could brag about it to those girls you keep hanging out with at the 7-Eleven."

Before Farshid had a chance to answer, the phone rang. Farshid grabbed it, presuming it would be one of the girls. Disappointed, he handed the phone to me, and I heard Sara's soft voice on the other end. She wanted to see me. Ehsan and Mahshid had left the apartment to go shopping in San Francisco. They would not be home all day.

I jumped in my car and sped to Ehsan's. Driving as fast as I could, I thought of Farshid getting a ticket. In that moment, I understood the need to speed.

Sara opened the door, and I could not believe my eyes. She was wearing a little makeup that enhanced her beauty. She was stunning. I was awestruck.

We walked over to a nearby park and, looking deep into each other's eyes, professed our love. My body felt on fire, not a fire with a burning sensation but one that lit me up with warmth and well-being.

After I dropped her off at the apartment, I kept sniffing my hands to breathe in the scent of her perfume. We arranged to meet up again, alone. She would have Soodi call Anahita to tell me where and when.

CHAPTER 18

THE AYATOLLAH

At San Jose City College, all one could hear among the Iranian students was "Death to the shah." Iranians from all walks of life were against him, the man who wanted his country to be as prosperous and modern as Western countries. The revolution was a unifying force among the poor, middle-class, and upper-class Iranian people. They all wanted Khomeini to topple the shah and his regime. Now the middle and upper classes were also being fooled by Khomeini and his false promises of a better future. This ayatollah, or Shiite religious leader, was now being called an imam. Up until now, there had always been only twelve imams, the Shiite religious leaders who were descendants of Mohammad. As Ehsan pointed out, no one questioned Khomeini's title of imam. Khomeini's supporters had declared him to be an imam even though no one could prove that he was a true descendant of the last imam. It was Mahdi, the twelfth Imam, who was going to be resurrected to bring justice to the world before the day of judgment. I wondered how a thirteenth imam would fit into the picture.

Khomeini was all over the news now, demanding that the shah step down and leave the country at once. I wondered why the shah didn't squash this so-called imam. On a microscale, it would be like

Farshid demanding that Behrouz leave our apartment—Farshid, a small nothing of a man, asking Behrouz, who held the lease, to leave. All Behrouz would have to do was wield his will to defeat Farshid and throw him out. Why was the shah not able to impose his will over Khomeini?

When my appointment came up at the DMV, Mehdi, my driving instructor, and Anahita came along to give me support. Following the driving examiner outside to my car, I glanced back and saw that Mehdi had diverted his eyes to the floor, as he was speaking to my sister. He might be a communist politically, but he was a decent man. He avoided talking about politics as conscientiously as he averted his eyes when he spoke to my sister. He was there for me when I needed him; therefore I had enormous respect for him.

I passed the test easily since I had been driving illegally for three months already. The examiner said that he had never seen a teen who drove so confidently.

Leaving the DMV with my temporary driver's license in hand, I got behind the steering wheel and yelled out, "Get in, friends! A licensed driver will escort you home."

We took Mehdi to his apartment.

"Good job, Borz," Mehdi shouted from his doorway. As he opened his front door, the rich smell of the Iranian stew abgoosht reached my nostrils and reminded me that I was starving. I wondered if abgoosht was all Mehdi and his comrades ever ate.

When I walked Anahita up to her apartment, I was surprised to see Farshid's little sister, Mehri, come out and greet us. She was back in the United States. They invited me in, and Anahita told Mehri that Soodi and Sara had also just arrived. A look of uneasiness momentarily flitted across Mehri's face. She asked when everyone could meet them. There was a question behind her question, but I could not tell what it was.

Anahita started filling Farah and Mehri in on all the girly details of Soodi and Sara, so I left and went home, thinking it would be more interesting listening to Farshid brag about his latest exploits than hearing the girls talk about what hairstyles Soodi and Sara were wearing.

Later that evening, I received a disturbing call from Mr. Abdollah Zadeh, Sara's father. He was a rich merchant who employed many people, including servants for his home. When he introduced himself on the phone, I got very worried, thinking he had learned of my love affair with his fifteen-year-old daughter. In a subdued voice, he first asked how I was doing. Then he changed the subject to current events.

"Did you hear that General Azhari is now the new prime minister? His Majesty had to change the prime minister again because of that crazy man in France. I'm sure you know that I am talking about Khomeini. Listen, Borz. Things are bad here in Iran. We are thinking of fleeing the country ourselves, but Ehsan is sending our twins, Soodi and Sara, home on an airplane in a couple of days. You must know that his wife, Mahshid, doesn't get along with them. I don't want my daughters to be sent back to Tehran. It's very unsafe now. There is a lot of unrest and fighting ... stray bullets ... The place is collapsing. I talked to Ehsan for an hour earlier, and he finally agreed that my daughters could stay in San Jose but only if they moved in with your sister Anahita. I already spoke with your parents, and they are amenable to that too.

"I know you are a smart and trustworthy boy, Borz. That is why I am calling you. I need your help. Please talk your sister Anahita into moving in with my daughters as soon as possible. Do whatever it takes. Then go speak to Ehsan immediately and tell him to find an apartment for my twins and your sister to share. I know that you have a car and are driving, so I may need you to take them to school if the apartment that Ehsan finds is not within walking distance.

"I'll find a way to thank you when I get to the United States. I don't want my daughters to come back to Tehran, and I'm willing to do anything to keep them away from here, at least until everything settles down. Can you help me, my son?"

I was thrilled to hear this important man begging me to save his daughters.

"Yes, sir. I will go speak to Anahita and Ehsan right away. I won't let your daughters get sent back. Trust me, sir."

He thanked me and hung up the phone. The word *trust* echoed in my ear. I'd asked him to trust me, but he did not know Sara's and my secret, that we loved each other to eternity and back.

I woke up Farshid, who had fallen asleep on the couch, so he could accompany me to Ehsan's. For some reason, I did not want to drive alone.

As Farshid got ready, I called Anahita. As soon as she heard that Soodi and Sara might be sent back if she did not move in with them, she agreed to the arrangement. She assured me that Farah would be okay with it since Mehri had just moved back and was now living with them, sharing a bedroom with Farah. If Anahita moved out, they could each have their own bedroom.

What luck, I thought, that everything was going to work out so that my sister would be living with my girlfriend.

Farshid and I arrived at Ehsan's around nine thirty. Ehsan motioned us in. Farshid entered the apartment first, as he always had to be first in everything. Behind Farshid's back, Ehsan gave me a look of disapproval. I knew he did not like Farshid, but that was not my concern at the moment. I launched into my story, saying I had talked to his father. Ehsan listened somewhat impatiently.

"Thank you and your sister for stepping up to help my sisters so they can stay in the United States. This is the best outcome. I will cancel their plane tickets and immediately start looking for an apartment."

I could hear crying behind a closed door. I turned my head toward the sound, and Ehsan explained, "Soodi and Sara are very upset that they have to go back to Iran so soon. They will be overjoyed when they hear of our plan."

I was able to hide my feeling of satisfaction that I had been instrumental in getting them to stay. All I said was "I will help move them in with my sister when you find an apartment."

Ehsan thanked me again, and Farshid and I left. On the way back home, Farshid told me how jealous he was.

"What do you mean? Why are you jealous?" I asked.

"You love this girl, and now she is in your control. Lucky bastard!"

In early November Jasmin called me and said that she'd arranged with the INS to transfer to a college in California in January. She had wanted to move in with Anahita but was aware of Soodi and Sara's situation. Instead, she arranged to share a place in Oakland with some friends she knew from Tehran. She would ask Anahita to move in with her the following summer. Anahita was ecstatic that our big sister was moving back to California.

Ehsan called me a couple of days later to let me know that he'd rented an apartment for his sisters and Anahita that would be available November 15. Not only had he put down the security deposit, but he had also paid the first three months of rent. That meant that Anahita and I could save the money we would pay for her part of the rent. Since I was constantly worried about money, that gave me some relief.

The girls' new apartment was in a beautiful gated community on Winchester Boulevard, on the border between San Jose and Campbell. It was a brand-new complex, designed with Mexican-style architecture. A lush landscape surrounded an inviting pool and Jacuzzi. Ehsan had rented a two-bedroom, two-bath corner suite. The twins took the master suite, and Anahita moved into the other bedroom.

Mr. Zadeh called me again to confirm that everything was working out. I assured him that Ehsan had rented an apartment for Soodi, Sara, and Anahita and that I would pick up his daughters every morning and take them to Santa Clara High School, where they were registered.

The apartment complex had a Campbell, California, address, but Ehsan did not report his sisters' move to the Santa Clara High School staff, as he knew they would be told they had to attend the local high school in Campbell. Ehsan knew that the high school and, more importantly, the INS did not need to know that the girls had changed addresses.

On moving day, Sara whispered in my ear that she wanted me to come over for dinner that evening. I wasn't sure what we would have for dinner, since none of the girls knew how to cook, but I was thrilled to get a chance to spend time with Sara without having to be under the gaze of our guardian, Ehsan.

I went home after moving everything into the new apartment to quickly shower before returning for dinner. Behrouz and his new girlfriend were just turning on some music when I opened the front door. Behrouz introduced me to her as his fiancée. I had met Zohreh before, as she was the other Borz's sister. Surprised at the sudden news, I asked Zohreh if her brother, Borz, knew. Behrouz explained that their parents had already talked. In fact, Zohreh's parents were en route for the upcoming engagement party.

Behrouz headed off my next question, which had to do with our apartment, since he was the only one on the lease. He said that he was not planning on leaving the apartment for at least a year, so I did not need to worry about getting a new roommate. He then shot me a look to leave the room and turned back to the cassette player. I had better things to do than watch the two of them dance intimately, as I had seen them do at a party. Sara was waiting for me, and I needed to get cleaned up.

As I was leaving, Farshid pulled up and asked me to see the new amplifier he had installed in his car. Laughing, he bragged that he'd written a check for the amplifier but had no money in his account, because he had moved it all to his sister's account. That way, he got the amplifier for free, because the check would bounce. He was seventeen years old and already honing his skills at becoming a crook.

I told him I had to leave and started walking toward my car. He looked at me jealously and said, "Are you going out with your relative? When can the rest of us meet this mysterious girl?"

"Maybe in another life!" I shouted back over my shoulder.

I just didn't trust him. He was one of the most jealous and competitive people I had ever known. He played life as a game of one-upmanship.

When I arrived at the apartment, Sara opened the door. Anahita was in the bathroom, fighting with her long, straight hair to get some curls to stay. Soodi was in the other bathroom, doing the same thing. Sara didn't have to do that, as her naturally wavy hair always appeared to be styled.

Sara and I had a few moments to ourselves. As we sat next to each other on the couch, I looked deep into her eyes, and my heart almost stopped beating. She wouldn't let me kiss her, but I could take her hand and caress its tenderness.

Soodi came into the living room and yelled, "Stop it, you lovebirds! I am hungry. Let's all go out to dinner."

The spell was broken, and we quickly scooted away from each other on the couch.

Going out to dinner two or three times a week became our routine. Sara and Soodi always offered to pay, but my ego never allowed it. In a few months my entire savings would be drained by the dinners, but I did not care, because I was with Sara.

In December 1978, it was becoming more and more clear that Iran's monarchy was going to end. Somehow the ayatollah's message was infiltrating almost everyone. Even Sara liked him. She wanted to pray like Muslims do and encouraged me to do the same. Even though I loved Sara, I could not do that for her. I just did not believe in it. I had been born Muslim, but my parents had never taken Islam seriously. Dad would sometimes drink whiskey during the holy month of Ramadan, the month of fasting from food and vices. There was no way I could just become religious or even pretend to be religious. To do so felt false, fraudulent.

Also, I saw how the ayatollah was quickly changing the social and political landscape of Iran. Like a pit bull that never lets go of its enemy and never tires of the fight, Khomeini relentlessly fought to oust his enemy, the shah. But ousting the shah was not his end goal. He was bloodthirsty. He had already assassinated the shah's character; now he wanted to kill the shah.

For the next two months, I picked up all three girls every morning. I dropped Sara and Soodi off at Santa Clara High School and then drove Anahita and me to either San Jose City College or Evergreen. Since our classes usually ended around two in the afternoon, that gave me plenty of time to pick up the twins from high school and drop them off at their apartment along with my sister. Ehsan had arranged that I tutor the twins in math, which I found delightful, making Sara dependent on me for her math grade.

Having her dependent on me was a way for me to feel I had the upper hand. Sara was a complicated girl who, I slowly and painfully learned, twisted facts into stories that worked in her favor. It was a roller-coaster relationship, where we would be coasting along just fine until, out of the blue, Sara would say something that would set me off.

We fantasized about getting married, and I would go home at night imagining what it would be like living with her and waking up to have morning tea with her. Then one day, when I whispered in her ear that I couldn't wait until we were married, she proclaimed in her matter-of-fact way that she could not marry me because my brother, Farhad, was married to her sister Salma. She claimed that her parents would be against our marriage because they felt it was inappropriate for two brothers to marry two sisters. They would be concerned, she explained, that if my brother and her sister divorced, it would put a strain on our relationship. Sara knew just how to pull problems out of thin air to confound me. We would argue over a whole dinner at what I would realize later, driving home, was an absurd aberration that Sara had concocted on the spot to cause contention.

The argument that we could not marry because her sister and my brother may divorce was a problematic but distorted presupposition. I approached life much differently than my older brother. For a wedding gift, Dad had endowed Farhad with a successful clothing boutique. Managing it provided Farhad with a steady and strong income. Salma's father had provided a nice home as a wedding gift. Farhad and Salma had not had to work their way up, as they had been given the means to live a very comfortable life from the day they'd married. Farhad had yet to deal with any kind of hardship. He never planned to live abroad. He was coping with the situation in Iran day by day.

This was not going to be my future, having my family set me up in business. I had already had to negotiate living and going to school in a foreign country and balancing a budget where each time I ran out of money, it was harder and harder for my family to send me more. Sara using the fact that her sister and my brother were married as the reason we could not get married was one way she could twist facts into a story that suited her. I was not my brother. If she really wanted to marry me, as I slowly would realize, she would stop making up reasons why we could not.

We often got into arguments like this and would stop talking for days, despite the fact that I had to pick her up every morning. The silent treatment was torturous until I reached out to make up with her. I would swallow my pride, talk myself into being apologetic, and try to make amends.

Sara never initiated an apology because she believed that men should beg women for their attention. She treated me like a pet and would extend her hand to pat my head only when I had begged and pleaded for forgiveness for a crime I had not committed.

The ups and downs were taking their toll on me. I started fantasizing about breaking up with her for good.

I noticed that she would sometimes watch other boys. Whenever I confronted her about how sincere she was about being my girlfriend, she would look at me with unblinking eyes in disbelief and convince me in a torrent of sincere-sounding sentences that she loved me more than anything and wanted to marry me. We would ride along smoothly for a few days, until she would twist the marriage thing around again, like a loose thread on her sweater that she habitually was drawn to, claiming that there was no way we could get married. And once again, we would argue until the silent treatment came down as heavy and as impenetrable as a garage door.

When we were coasting, enjoying being together, she would often drop a disparaging declaration against someone I knew, like Mehri, who was good friends with Anahita. Mehri was cute and confident. Sara hated the way Mehri carried herself so assuredly. I liked Mehri and could not stand listening to Sara insult her. Sara would also comment offhandedly that Anahita wore provocative clothes, a statement that was false and was only uttered to aggravate me.

The on-again, off-again game with Sara was wrenching. Soon, the off-again periods stretched longer than the on-again periods. I began to feel that our relationship was doomed and started feeling a sense of relief during our silent periods, as I did not have to defend my friends, my family, or myself. It would take courage to actually break up with Sara, to stand my ground and not get looped back into her Gordian knot of illogic.

As Sara and I were slowly and painfully breaking up, Iran was breaking apart on a much more massive scale. General Azhari was appointed prime minister on November 8, 1978. He had been the chief of staff of Iran's military services and chose military men for the majority of his cabinet positions, making it the first time that there had been a military government since 1953. But it didn't last. Azhari resigned less than two months later, after suffering a heart attack. Two weeks before his heart attack, he warned the US ambassador to Iran, William Sullivan, "You must know this, and you must tell it to your government. This country is lost because the shah cannot make up his mind."

Unaware that Azhari had warned the United States of the shah's impending doom, the shah allowed Azhari to flee the country. Yet the shah felt he needed to round up some scapegoats as a last-ditch effort to bolster his position as the rightful head of state. He jailed the illustrious former prime minister Amir Abbas Hoveyda and the former head of SAVAK General Nematollah Nassiri, along with almost sixty other former officials. General Nassiri was called from his post as ambassador to Pakistan to attend a meeting in Tehran, and he went, unaware that he would be summarily arrested and jailed. Misguided, the shah thought he could show empathy with the angry mobs by arresting officials who had served him or were part of his government. It completely backfired. Instead, the arrest of the government officials validated the mistrust of his regime and stoked, instead of smothered, the sentiments against him.

He also proved that when push came to shove, he would heartlessly push his way to the top and shove his trusted advisers off a cliff. He never could explain away such an act of ruthless desperation.

His last attempt to create a civilian government was to appoint Dr. Shapour Bakhtiar, a former leader of a moderate, democratic-leaning opposition party, the National Front, as prime minister. Dr. Bakhtiar's job was to create a civilian government, to put a new face on Iran control and move away from the military government of his predecessor, General Azhari. During his short reign, Dr. Bakhtiar relaxed martial law, removed the censorship of newspapers, and released political prisoners. He planned on holding elections to decide the fate of the monarchy. But it was all too late. None of these measures could reverse the tide of the uprising, which had built for twelve months and had one goal in mind: replace the monarchy with the mullah Khomeini.

Dr. Bakhtiar's fatal mistake was to let the shah's nemesis back into the country. Ruhollah Khomeini boarded an Air France jet on February 1, 1979, two weeks after the shah had left the country, ostensibly for vacation, on January 16. Newspapers around the world did not swallow the story of the shah going on holiday. Some of them exposed the truth. "The shah of Iran has fled the country following months of increasingly violent protests against his regime." "Shah of Iran flees into exile." "Shah Mohammed Reza Pahlavi and his wife, Empress Farah, left Tehran and flew to Aswan in Egypt." "Opposition to the shah has become united behind the Muslim traditionalist movement led by Iran's main spiritual leader, Ayatollah Ruhollah Khomeini, from exile in France."

Khomeini's motorcade was met by millions of supporters as it slithered through the streets of Tehran. When asked by American journalist Peter Jennings, who had accompanied the exiled leader of the opposition on his flight back to Tehran, how he felt about returning to Iran, Khomeini uttered one word: "Nothing." Much discourse would be spent in the coming years on what the mullah meant by that, if it was his religious nonattachment perception or if he was an unfeeling human being.

Articles supporting the return of the exiled eminence burst with praise, making claims such as "Opposition to the shah has become united behind the Muslim traditionalist movement led by Iran's main spiritual leader, Ayatollah Ruhollah Khomeini, from exile in France."

Ehsan called to commiserate with me on the evening of Khomeini's return.

"Here it is, Borz. Did you see the BBC headlines? Have you been following the news on that rag? They have propped up Khomeini as some kind of Eastern mystic, as if he cares a rat's ass about anyone other than himself. They handed him his fame by making him a household name. He took advantage of it and played the press, acting like a religious cleric when, in fact, he is nothing but a power-hungry politician.

"Britain is a country that claims to support human rights, yet they are standing behind a cleric in pursuit of theocracy! And here the BBC claims to support free speech. How can they honor the return of that mullah, who wants to take away all rights, including free speech? It was the free speech of the protesters that brought him back and that is handing him the government. Now mark my words, Borz: there will soon be no free speech in Iran. The mullah wants to wind the clock back hundreds of years. How can the BBC and the West not see that coming?

"And it is utterly unbelievable that Carter and his cronies believe that Khomeini will create a democracy in Iran. Have they not been listening to him? Or are they just basting together news briefings from the BBC? If that's the case, then that's the reason Carter and Ambassador Sullivan think Khomeini is the next Gandhi and will bring peace to our homeland. I don't know if you have been reading the American papers, Borz, but they describe Khomeini as a moderate and a progressive. They, along with the BBC, are accomplices in promoting Khomeini's messages and destroying the monarchy. The Americans pretend to back the shah, but they are propping up Khomeini, claiming he will calm the protests and take back control of the country. Sure, he'll do that, but it's going to be a very different country when he finally does take over. I'm warning you, Borz. There are dark days ahead."

CHAPTER 19

BREAKING UP

Seemingly overnight, the country where I had grown up, where my mother and sisters could wear the latest Italian fashions, where my father could run his catering business and restaurant without the paranoid interference of a fascist government, was gone. Khomeini won the kangaroo court election, where there was a yes/no vote on whether Iran should become an Islamic republic. It was not as simple for Khomeini as just winning the election; he had to crush all his dissidents, including the communists, who had backed and supported him during the revolution, so that he could become the supreme ruler. The next two years were an ugly time for Iran. The cancer of Khomeini's rule spread into all factions of life, limiting education, restricting women, strangling the rights of everyone, and exterminating those who violently or even meekly protested. I thought Ehsan's warning of dark days ahead meant that things would get a little more difficult in the transition, but I assumed that once the revolution was over, calm, not calamity, would take over the country.

Khomeini cut off the flow of money for students abroad, spiraling me and other Iranian students I knew into poverty. I grieved for my homeland, lost now, on the other side of the world. It was like the country I had known had died, as it was no longer accessible to me.

The people who took over my country looked as if they had all been cast from the same depressing mold, with their unshaven, long faces and their worn suits or typical disheveled mullah garb. Originality, personality, and differentiation retreated to the underground. The new leaders spoke intimidatingly, using fear tactics as their communication device. I couldn't imagine ever going back to my country with these people in charge. My plan to come to the United States to get an education and return home to Iran to secure a good job was now irrevocably changed. I now realized I had to make a home here—not a temporary home as a student, but a permanent home as an immigrant.

I was thoroughly disappointed that the shah had not done much to squelch the opposition. He'd abdicated his position and left people like my family to fend for themselves. The shah hadn't wanted bloodshed, but because of his impotence, there was more bloodshed at the hands of the people who replaced him. Khomeini's rise to power came about by mere luck. This was how I'd always felt about that man's success in taking full control of my country. I felt that we were now part of a lost herd, untethered from our original principles of human rights and Persian glory, as set out by Cyrus the Great.

After the revolution, I became dirt poor and often had to ask Ehsan, who was also struggling financially, for help. I, along with all the other Iranian students who had gone overseas to get an education, was forced to take a seat on the roller-coaster ride at a sick Khomeini-influenced carnival. From abroad, we witnessed the destruction of our families, homes, and businesses, and we experienced poverty as we had not ever known. We had to come to terms with the fact that we might not be able to return to our country of origin, and if we did, it would have metamorphosed into something unrecognizable. I, along with many other Iranians, felt the anxiety and disconnect of becoming displaced. We weren't sure what was going to happen to us, to our families, and to our country.

At times, my finances were so bad that I had to live with five or six roommates in downtrodden two-bedroom, one-bathroom apartments. I sold my car to pay for my tuition and took a job at a 7-Eleven to support myself, working the graveyard shift so I could still attend classes. The 7-Eleven was located in one of San Jose's toughest neighborhoods, and I came close to getting held up and shot many times. Eventually, I quit the 7-Eleven and started working in restaurants. Because of my financial difficulties, I could only afford to take six units at a time. I felt isolated but became self-sufficient. Working and going to school took up almost all my time, and consequently I became a loner. I spent my free time reading everything I could get my hands on about the history of Iran and the revolution. I was particularly interested in Cyrus the Great, who had been king of Persia 2,500 years ago. He was famous for, among other things, allowing the exiled Jews to return to Babylon and had been tolerant of the customs and religions of the lands he'd conquered. As the ayatollah decried the very existence of Israel, I realized that he was not only determined to destroy all cultural progress in Iran but was also isolating the country and creating hostility with Israel, an extremely important and strategic regional neighbor. The question of how we could have fallen so far from the vision of an ancient king from 2,500 years ago haunted me.

CHAPTER 20

AS ADULTS

After graduating from college, I worked in IT, starting at Intel as a product engineer. At that time, I changed my name to Brian, an Anglo name that I liked. I changed my name because Borz sounded like a herd of boars and I liked the sound of Brian.

I met my wife, Nadia, at a travel agency where she worked. When I walked into the office to inquire about an airplane ticket, she looked up from her desk at me, and I immediately fell in love with her light-brown eyes. After repeatedly asking her out on a date, she finally acquiesced.

My sister Jasmin didn't move to Oakland until the spring of 1979. She attended Holy Names University and lived in a lovely apartment in the Oakland Hills. Dad bought her a new 1978 Pontiac Sunbird when she moved back to California, and this time she chose a brown exterior, instead of taxi orange. Anahita moved to Oakland to live with Jasmin in the summer of that year. Oakland was not too far away from where I was living, but when they both moved to Los Angeles in 1980, I really felt alone. I had no immediate family around.

Jasmin finished school at the University of Southern California, graduating with a degree in psychology, and then went on to get her PhD in psychology many years later. She and her husband, a successful Iranian businessman, moved to Texas in 2001. As Jasmin matured, she proved to be there for her family in tough times. She was no longer the tumultuous teenager that Anahita and I had lived with when we'd first come over from Iran. Throughout the years, she has supported her siblings financially whenever she could. She turned out to be a person I could count on as a loving friend and mentor.

My twin, Anahita, moved with Jasmin to Los Angeles and obtained a degree in language arts and American literature from the University of Southern California. She married young and had two children. After she divorced her husband, she became a successful insurance broker.

My brother, Farhad, and his wife, Salma, moved to the United States in October 1982. Farhad had to flee the country because of a song that he'd written against the government. Unlike the last time he had been arrested for writing a song for Dariush, he could not rely on my father to bail him out this time. He chose freedom over fortune and left all his assets to the Islamic Republic of Iran (IRI) in order to escape.

Farhad divorced Salma in 1984. He now lives in Los Angeles.

I did not have to worry about how Farhad's divorce would affect Sara's and my relationship, as Sara was no longer in my life. Sara and I broke up in 1982 when I could no longer put up with the mind games that she always played with me. Also, prior to our breakup, I found out that she was seeing another guy who was interested in marrying her. That was the final straw.

My parents moved to the United States one month after Farhad, in November 1982. They entered the United States through Spain, knowing they would never go back. The IRI had not bothered my father, as he was just a restaurateur and a caterer. They had even offered to have him continue his catering services with the new leadership, but he hated them and had refused to work for them.

In Spain, he went to the American embassy and showed a photograph of himself posing with the shah. They offered immediate asylum to him and Mom.

Just like Farhad, my dad left everything behind, including his businesses. He had been an extremely wealthy man in Iran, being the owner of the largest restaurant in the capital and of a very successful catering company. Between 1973 and 1979, the shah had paid Dad's catering company the equivalent of $17,000 a month.

Dad was only able to sell one of his homes before leaving and used that money to purchase a small restaurant in San Jose. But he sold the small restaurant a year later and moved to Los Angeles to live in the largest Iranian community outside of Iran. My father never went back to visit Iran, because he considered it a betrayal to his personal values. My parents both converted to Christianity in 1994. They made many friends with members of the Iranian Christian Church. After retiring at the age of sixty-six, Dad spent most of his free time in the Iranian libraries in Westwood, California. He passed away in February 2011. About two-thirds of the hundred people who attended his funeral were his Persian Jewish friends. Mom now lives alone in Los Angeles.

Every Iranian's life, no matter where they were, who they were, or what side they were on, dramatically changed. Rural folks gained the most in terms of finance, position, and power. The ayatollah depended on the backwoods bucolic brood, having built his regime with their support. In return, he allowed them to gain power and wealth by occupying key posts in the government. Everyone else received nothing. Mainstream middle-class and upper-class Iranians lost everything. Thousands lost their lives.

My friend Mehdi, the communist, waited until Iran transitioned from monarchy to Islamic republic before he returned, feeling victorious. He headed back in 1980, thinking he would be key in rebuilding the future of Iran. Once he landed and connected with some of his comrades, he shockingly discovered that the new government was expediting the execution of its communist allies at a hair-trigger rate. Many of Mehdi's friends were executed in the first year of the IRI, the very regime they'd fought hard to establish. Mehdi kept mum about his political leanings and became part of the silent majority. When I reconnected with him years later through Facebook, I realized that the mercurial Mehdi had changed from a consummate communist to an everyday Iranian and had involuntarily joined the ranks of the unemployed. His punishment for planting the poisonous seeds of revolution and returning to his motherland was to live out a long death sentence in the psychological prison of the Islamic Republic of Iran, void of freedoms. Most of his comrades from San Jose remained in the democratic United States and became successful business owners. They did not have to reap the rotten fruit of the seeds they'd planted in their homeland.

After receiving his master's degree in civil engineering from San Jose State, Ehsan opened a civil engineering company with two partners. He borrowed money from his father, Abdollah Zadeh, to start the business. Abdollah had moved to the United States in 1980, thinking it would be a temporary situation. He never liked living abroad. He missed Tehran and found the courage to go back in 1984. Because he had lost his very successful business by moving to the United States, he eventually had to ask Ehsan to wire him the money that he owed him. At that time, Ehsan was struggling financially to launch his company. He was in no position to pay his father back, and that strained their relationship. Two years later, the former great merchant Abdollah Zadeh passed away before reconciling with his son. Ehsan fell into a depression over the loss of his estranged father. Later, he found solace in Christianity. Ehsan and his business partners became devoted Christians. He and his wife, Mahshid, who also converted to Christianity, now live in one of the affluent suburbs of San Francisco and are doing well financially and spiritually.

Nassir never married his Chinese girlfriend, as she moved to Canada. That speed bump in his happy-go-lucky life did not deter him. He fell in love with and married an Iranian woman, had two children, and settled down in the Bay Area, becoming a vice president of a semiconductor company. His infectiously happy spirit never waned.

After the revolution took hold, I had no interest in returning to Iran for many years. Not only did the revolution strangle my country, its effects strangled those of us who were expats in the United States and elsewhere.

I did make one trip back to Iran with my mother to see relatives in 2005. It would be the only trip back for me. At the time, I was a little afraid of being caught and jailed by the IRI because of some blogs I had posted on the Internet that did not put Iran in the best light.

When I returned, a mullah named Khatami (similar to the name Khomeini) was stepping down as president, as he had termed out. Mahmoud Ahmadinejad had won the election, and there was much talk on the streets of Ahmadinejad's planned crackdowns. Hearing these rumors, I was glad that I would be returning to the United States before he took office.

After twenty-nine years of being away, I felt like a tourist in what had once been my home. Street names had been changed. The gray buildings looked dull and downtrodden. Passersby wore expressions of defeat and surrender. Almost thirty years of suppression and loss of freedom stained everything, from people's downcast expressions to the muted businesses and city streets. I had no friends to look up, as three decades of time had dissolved any connections I'd had with them. My visits with the few family members who had not made it out were as stilted as stopping in on strangers. I felt shortness of breath the whole time, as if the life force of oxygen itself had been put behind a veil. The awareness that Iran could now claim to have one of the highest rates of pollution, prostitution, and addiction made me sick to my stomach with grief, as I felt as if my country had died.

Riding in a cab to the market one day, the driver played Journey's song "Lights." Hearing an American band singing of loneliness made me long for my home in California so much that I broke into tears in the back of the cab. The irony of it was that when I'd heard a song from my own country by Dariush twenty-nine years ago in San Jose, it had made me homesick for Tehran, where I now was. Riding in a cab listening to "Well, my friend, I'm lonely too / I want to get back to my city by the bay," it seemed as if the unfamiliar streets of my hometown had turned their back on me. Both times I'd felt deep homesickness when I'd heard songs from the opposite sides of my life and the furthest points from each other in the world.

CHAPTER 21

THE LAST DAYS OF THE SHAH

The shah had a sad and painful journey from the time he was run out of Iran up until the time of his death in the summer of 1980. He desperately sought political refuge and medical assistance for cancer in Egypt, Morocco, the Bahamas, Mexico, New York, Texas, Panama, and back to Egypt. He first went to Egypt in the spring of 1979 and was welcomed warmly by President Anwar Sadat, but he decided to go to Morocco after only a few weeks. King Hassan of Morocco, who used to get his lunch money from the shah, had made a friendly gesture and invited him for a visit. Shortly after the shah's arrival, King Hassan's aides ordered him to leave. King Hussein of Jordan also had depended on the shah for financial support, but he never invited the shah to his country, even when the shah was in desperate need.

Instead of helping the shah, Carter's administration placed their bets on the wrong horse, Khomeini. If it weren't for Sadat's last-minute rescue of the shah, the Panamanians and White House Chief of Staff Hamilton Jordan would have probably extradited the shah back to Tehran. The dictator of Panama at that time, General Omar Torrijos Herrera, known for being a professional gambler, among other ignominious things, wanted to play his "king" card, the shah. Torrijos was secretly negotiating with Tehran for possible extradition of the shah in order to help end the Iran hostage crisis and thus improve Jimmy Carter's changes of getting reelected for a second term. For his own country's sake, Torrijos knew there was no chance for negotiating a better term for the Panama Canal if Ronald Reagan became president. But the Iran hostage crisis foiled that plan, and Carter's chances for a second term evaporated.

The shah passed away from cancer on July 27, 1980, in Cairo, Egypt, at sixty-one years old. I've never been able to understand why the shah's Western allies did not back him, a pro-Western leader, and instead chose to support the uprisings and the "holy man" Khomeini. The Western allies never allowed the shah to enter their countries because they wanted to keep their options open with Tehran. The shah's circle of friends, when he most needed them, was reduced to Richard Nixon, Henry Kissinger, Anwar El Sadat, Nelson Rockefeller, Frank Sinatra, and President Carter's national security adviser, Zbigniew Kazimierz Brzezinski. Richard Nixon called Jimmy Carter's treatment of the shah "one of the black pages of the American foreign policy history." I felt they were men of honor for standing by their friend till his death.

The shah was psychologically and emotionally dependent on the support of his nation and the US government. When both turned against him, he became terrified and did not know how to deal with the situation. Iran and the entire region fell into a downward spiral of fundamental Islamic ideologies after that.

Before leaving his country for the final time, the shah said, "If I leave, Iran will go down. If Iran goes down, the Middle East will go down, and if the Middle East goes down, the world will suffer." History has proved that his prophecies were true. The Middle East and the world now suffer from atrocious terrorists such as ISIS and al-Qaeda, to the point that countries like the United States have no option but to get in bed with the mullahs in Iran in order to balance the power in the region.

CHAPTER 22

THE HOSTAGE CRISIS AND THE IRANIAN REVOLUTION

Jimmy Carter's foreign policy decisions marked the beginning of the end of the Persian glory and the shah's vision of a great civilization and propelled the rise of Islamic power in the region. He started by sending mixed signals to the government of Iran that created confusion on how to deal with the uprisings. When it was too late to control the situation, Carter invited the leaders of the UK, Germany, and France to a summit on the French Republic island of Guadeloupe in 1979 and asked them to agree to back the overthrow of the shah. He later sent General Huyser to Tehran to encourage the Iranian military leaders to support the shah's exile. Many years later, General Huyser divulged the fact that Carter had deceived him by giving him erroneous information. He said Carter was responsible for the ouster of the shah. Some American scholars, such as Mike Evans, have accused Carter of sending hundreds of millions of dollars to Khomeini in increments while he was in exile in Paris. The information is backed by a former CIA operative. If this information is true, Carter basically financed the overthrow of the shah, resulting in the regional disorder that we are experiencing today. He continues to support Hamas and other terrorist groups around the world. It's hard for me to understand why Jimmy Carter is so obsessed with the rise of radical Islamic groups in the region and the weakening of Israel.

Shortly after the shah's admission to New York Hospital, pro-Khomeini students invaded the US embassy on November 4, 1979, and took fifty-two American diplomats and citizens hostage for 444 days. The ayatollah quickly showed his true nature to the presidents of the United States, France, and Germany, who had stood behind him during the transition. Jimmy Carter's incompetence in handling the hostage crisis cost him his second term as president. He lost the election to Ronald Reagan, who had threatened to bomb Iran if the hostages weren't released. The hostages were released and boarded a plane just as Reagan was delivering his inaugural address, on January 20, 1981.

The hostage crisis created a bad situation for Iranians in the United States. I personally paid for the terrorists' actions when an angry, ignorant mob beat me one night. It made me afraid—afraid to admit to anyone where I was from, afraid to speak Persian in public places. Some Iranians preferred the term *Persian* for this reason and still do, as the ignorance of many Americans sometimes distinguishes Persian from Iranian. Many of my friends were deported with no clear explanation. The INS summoned me and every other Iranian I knew to have our mug shots taken within seventy-two hours of the start of the hostage crisis. The INS treated us like suspects during the crisis.

Three years after the hostage crisis ended, the situation began to normalize. I no longer felt as afraid and was not discriminated against for being Iranian. The Western media described the Iranian Revolution as a populist, nationalist, and Islamic movement. The Western world believed the shah's economic programs were too ambitious, resulting in anger over a sharp economic contraction in the late 1970s. They also believed that the other shortcomings of the shah's regime contributed to the revolution. Many Iranians missed the fact that the Western world was angry at the shah for damaging their fragile economies by quadrupling the price of oil. Everyone ignored the Western media's role in making the ayatollah a hero.

The Islamic Republic of Iran turned out to be a nightmare nobody had predicted. A pro-Western semiabsolute monarchy was replaced with an anti-Western authoritarian theocracy based on the concept of *velayat-e faqih*, that a supreme Islamic leader, or jurist, of political law provide full guardianship over the people. For Khomeini and his cronies, it meant enforcing the law of Khomeini, the man who had overthrown the shah to make himself a dictator and who had appointed himself as the supreme leader.

Upon his arrival, Khomeini ordered the people not to use the term *democratic*, because it was a Western value. He gave the pro-democracy liberals, communists, and other parties who had backed him their first slap of disappointment. But there were more to come. Khomeini quickly moved in to close several dozen newspapers and magazines that opposed his ideas of theocratic rule by jurists. He claimed that the people would have complete freedom to have their own opinions at the same time that he was crushing all opposing factions. He and his supporters overpowered any native insurgencies and consolidated power by 1982.

Khomeini's quotes and speeches were mostly comic. In one speech he proclaimed, "A university that is not the university is not a university." In another speech he alleged, "Economy is for donkeys." Some of Khomeini's quotes were downright disturbing. In one quote Khomeini proclaimed, "A man can have sex with animals such as sheep, cows, camels and so on. However, he should kill the animal after he has his orgasm. He should not sell the meat to the people in his own village; however, selling the meat to the village next door should be fine." Khomeini proved to be sadistic when he said, "A man can marry a girl younger than nine years of age, even if the girl is still a baby being breastfed. A man, however, is prohibited from having intercourse with a girl younger than nine, yet other sexual acts such as foreplay, rubbing, kissing and sodomy are allowed."

This atrocious man, who was named *Time*'s Man of the Year in 1979 for his "international influence and virtual face of Islam," finally died of natural causes on June 3, 1989, in Tehran. Besides the destruction of Iran, his legacies include support of the American hostage takers and the fatwa he issued calling for the death of the British Indian novelist Salman Rushdie. Khomeini always referred to the United States as "the Great Satan." He was criticized for these acts and for human rights violations of Iranians, but he never paid for his crimes.

I was always captivated by the evil character of Khomeini and took it upon myself to study his upbringing. I wanted to learn about his roots because of the article that had inflamed the uprising. Researching his background, I discovered that he had been born in Iran but that his Persian ancestors had migrated to Northern India in the eighteenth century. His grandfather left India in the early part of the nineteenth century for a pilgrimage to Najaf, Iraq, which, ironically, was where Khomeini would later live in exile for thirteen years. Khomeini's grandfather never went back to India, but nine years later, he returned to Iran and settled in the village of Khomein. Khomeini's grandfather was known as Mostafa Hindi, meaning Mostafa the Indian. The ayatollah himself used to sign some of his poems as "Hindi." This explained the article that the shah had released.

Sayyed Ali Hosseini Khamenei, whose name is similar to Khomeini, is the second and current supreme leader of Iran. He was trained by the KGB and is a known terrorist in the world. His power is equal to absolute monarchy, allowing him to have full control over all aspects of life. In the post-revolutionary government of Iran, the president has some jurisdiction over internal matters, but the real political power lies with the supreme leader. Khamenei prides himself on continuing Khomeini's legacy in being the supreme leader.

After the revolution, human rights groups estimated the number of people killed or imprisoned to be fifteen thousand to twenty thousand. In the first three months, members of the old system, senior generals, and about two hundred other civilian officials were executed for various drummed-up crimes to secure power by eliminating the danger of opposition. There were sham trials without defense attorneys or jurors where the indicted were not given any chance to defend themselves. Khomeini preferred to identify the accused and annihilate them as expeditiously as possible. The prisoners were sentenced by the revolutionary chief justice, Sadegh Khalkhali, who earned a reputation as a hanging judge. By January 1980, more than five hundred members of the old regime had been executed. Among those executed was Amir Abbas Hoveyda, the former popular prime minister of Iran.

The IRI perpetrated greater crimes against other forms of opposition. The People's Mujahedin of Iran guerrillas came under attack in February 1980. About ten thousand members of the People's Mujahedin were executed in 1988. But the worst atrocities of the regime were committed during the war with Iraq. Shortly after securing his power, Khomeini wanted to export his revolution to neighboring countries. Iran and Iraq had a long history of border disputes that had been resolved by the shah and Saddam Hussein, but when the ayatollah seized power, he created fears that the Iranian Revolution would stimulate an uprising among Iraq's repressed Shia majority. Iraq hoped to take advantage of Iran's postrevolution disorder and attacked without warning by way of air and land on September 22, 1980. The war finally ended in August 1988, making it the longest conventional war of the twentieth century. One million Iranians died, and Iraq lost 250,000 to 500,000 soldiers.

The Khomeini regime moved quickly to replace SAVAK with a new and more evil institution called the Revolutionary Guards. Today, the Ministry of Intelligence of the Islamic Republic of Iran conducts acts of horror beyond the understanding of the civilized world. For years, this organization has been providing financial aid, weapons, intelligence, and logistics to the terrorists in Lebanon and Palestine. They have supported Hezbollah and Hamas in launching terror attacks against Israel and other countries.

Most of the IRI's opposition in Europe were brutally murdered. The first victim was Shahriar Shafiq, the son of Princess Ashraf Pahlavi, twin sister of the shah of Iran. Agents of the IRI assassinated him in Paris on December 7, 1979, shooting him twice in the head. The most famous victim of the IRI, however, was Dr. Shapour Bakhtiar, the last prime minister the shah had appointed as a final attempt to save the monarchy. Bakhtiar fled Iran shortly after Khomeini seized power. Bakhtiar was the most prominent and credible opposition to the IRI. He was based in Paris and led the National Movement of Iranian Resistance. The IRI issued a death sentence for him. He escaped the first assassination attempt by a group of three attackers in his home, but then one of the IRI's most notorious agents, Fereydoun Boyer-Ahmadi, gained his trust by serving in his party for almost five years. Boyer-Ahmadi brought two other assassins, Mohammad Azadi and Ali Vakili Rad, to Bakhtiar's home. The three men murdered Bakhtiar and his secretary, Soroush Katibeh, with common kitchen knives. Mohammad Azadi escaped back to Iran with Bakhtiar's Rolex watch to give to Iran's intelligence minister at the time, Ali Fallahian, as a souvenir.

The IRI has committed similar crimes against humanity that are summarized in what scholars have called the *chain murders* or *serial murders* of Iran. These were a series of murders and disappearances from 1988 to 1998 of Iranian intellectuals who had been critical of the IRI. The total number of casualties at the hands of the IRI is believed to be around fifteen thousand to twenty-five thousand. The IRI has assassinated more than eighty writers, translators, poets, political activists, and ordinary citizens by violent and torturous methods, including deliberate car crashes, stabbings, injections to simulate heart attacks, and head beatings. The serial murders came to light when Dariush Forouhar; his wife, Parvaneh Eskandari Forouhar; and three dissident writers were murdered in the span of two months in late 1998. Dariush Forouhar was another prominent and credible opposer of the IRI.

The United Nations believes that the violations of human rights by the IRI is far worse than under the old system. There are countless reports of torture, imprisonment of nonconformists, and the murder of political figures. Censorship is the norm, and it runs deep. No books or magazines are published, no movies are shown, and no cultural organization can be established without the permission of the Ministry of Culture and Islamic Guidance. All forms of popular music are banned. Men and women are still not allowed to dance or swim with each other in public. They are separated on buses and trains. Iran is now a mass graveyard of intellectuals, cultural and political figures, and innocents. It's a mentally diseased society with ten suicides per day and over ten million drug addicts. There are reports that more than ten thousand children are physically and/or sexually abused in Iran on a daily basis, and official reports show more than twenty million cases of similar abuse against women each year. More than ten million people suffer from depression, and about thirty million Iranians are unemployed.

The existing currency in Iran represents the true picture of Iran's economic decay. The Iranian rial, with a daunting picture of the ayatollah, is worth close to nothing. Ten Iranian rials equals one Iranian toman. Most Iranians use tomans as the main currency, even though the official currency is rial. During the shah's regime, seven tomans equaled one US dollar. Now three thousand tomans add up to one dollar. The currency has been devalued over

450 times. To make things worse, the Iranian currency is no longer part of the world index of currencies, meaning that Iranian rials cannot be exchanged for other currencies. Today, Iranian paper money is worth less than toilet paper.

CHAPTER 23
TEN FACTORS

The IRI is an efficient system of suppression with expertise in psychological oppression. The regime labels its opponents as undesirable. Khomeini and his regime have deprived Iranians of their basic rights, such as the right to hold free elections, the right to protest, the right to assemble, freedom of speech, religious choice, sexual freedom, and gender equality. The mullahs have become oppressors who torture Iranians with an unprecedented level of cruelty.

I have been trying to find the answers to questions such as, Why did our codes of honor disappear? How did we make the transition from the shah's Literacy Corps to Khomeini's Islamic armies of the saviors? Why did Iran have to go through these deep cultural changes to a new Islamic ideology? Why did we have to set these new standards of corruption and anarchy? I have found ten equal factors that lined up and played in Khomeini's favor to allow him to rise to power. The most important factor was the shah's refusal to have Khomeini hanged when he had the chance. The shah was a democratic. He had been educated in Switzerland and was schooled in Western democracy. He was not perfect, but he avoided executing the opposition as much as possible. In the 1960s, the shah had full control of the country and the power to eliminate a man who would ultimately be his demise. The shah did not execute Khomeini, because he did not want to kill a religious man.

The second factor relates to freedom of speech, even for Khomeini. If the shah had allowed Khomeini to speak freely in public, instead of being exiled, and say why he was against the regime, most people would have probably laughed at him. The fact is the ayatollah was against women's rights, the right to vote, distribution of land, the practice of other religions, and many other things. Iranians didn't know what the issue was between the ayatollah and the shah for many years, until they were deep into the darkness of the IRI. It was too late then to ask why they should support a man like Khomeini.

The shah raising the price of oil was the third factor. His act created many enemies in the West, most notoriously, the United Kingdom. These enemies took revenge on him as soon as they could.

The government of the United States was the fourth important factor in the Iranian Revolution gaining so much ground that it ultimately overthrew the shah. Jimmy Carter and the good ole country boys around him had never liked the shah because the shah had financially supported Republican candidates in the past. They saw it as an intervention in American politics by a man who was supposed to follow their lead, not the other way around.

The fifth factor was the big role the UK government's and the BBC's support of the ayatollah played in propping up Khomeini as the next leader of Iran. The Brits publicly supported Khomeini and brought him into the spotlight.

The sixth factor relates to the shah's uncertainty and confusion on how to deal with the uprising. He made many mistakes during that period. The shah's request that Saddam deport Khomeini from Iraq, for example, was a bad move. It resulted in having the evil man in the spotlight as the "holy man." The shah committed other mistakes by letting the uprisings get out of control.

The seventh factor was the ambassadors of the United States and the UK. They both showed ill will toward the shah. The two countries gave bad advice to the shah for many years because they were only interested in economic trading with Iran.

The eighth factor relates to the strange marriage of communism and Islamic fundamentalism. This unity gave a lot of momentum, force, and followers as well as a structure for the shah's opposition to succeed. The communists were highly organized and trained in guerrilla warfare, mostly by the government of Syria.

The ninth factor relates to the article that the shah released against Khomeini, disputing his origins. This action backfired on the shah. The only thing that the article did was give Khomeini more attention and press. The shah should have ignored him and not given him so much attention.

The tenth and, in my opinion, the most important factor relates to the shah's colossal sense of insecurity. He had deprived Iran of any viable opposition against him. All the men who were educated, intelligent, and independent thinkers were either exiled or under house arrest. This created a vacuum in the Iranian opposition leadership, hence paving the road for the maniacal Khomeini and his people to organize and give him more power. Iranians proved that if they don't like someone, such as the shah, they are willing to subject themselves to the shortsighted choice of a much worse fate, like Ayatollah Khomeini.

CHAPTER 24
CHILDREN OF CYRUS

Setting aside the ten factors that led to the Iranian Revolution, I still continue to wonder how a man like Khomeini, who believed Islam should encompass all aspects of life, could take full control of a great civilization and create a state of decay. Our ancestor, Cyrus the Great, who was the ruler of the Persian Empire, freed the Jews from Babylon and sent them to their motherland, Israel. But the IRI continues to embarrass the Persians on the world stage. One of the latest Iranian presidents, Ahmadinejad, declared that Israel, a sovereign state with so many intellectuals and contributions to science, must be annihilated. But Israel is a friend of Iranians, while most Arabs are the natural enemies of Iran. Just for reference, Israel conducted an operation against the strongest country of the Arab world, Iraq, when Saddam was at war with Iran. They bombed Saddam's nuclear plants and other strategic locations in the early 1980s. Israel had goodwill toward Iran until the mullahs took power and started denying the very right of the country to exist. Even today, the government of Israel supports the Iranian people more than other countries do. They are the true friends of the Persians, dating back to Cyrus the Great. All Iranians should respect the right of Israel to exist, especially in a region that is so hostile to them. But the current government of Iran likes to get in bed with the Palestinians, who the Iranian taxpayers are paying to support. Iran helped rebuild Lebanon after its war with Israel while its own cities needed upgraded infrastructure.

I have been asking myself, who are the true children of Cyrus? The mullahs are absolutely not the true children of Cyrus. In my relentless effort to find answers, another question continues to haunt me: How can the West negotiate a nuclear deal with a government that should not be trusted? I have one possible explanation. The elimination of the shah's regime destabilized the entire region. The West lost a true ally. Now they have to depend on the rulers of countries such as Saudi Arabia and Pakistan as friends. History has proven that the rulers of these countries can never truly be trusted. The Saudis have supported ISIS, and the Pakistanis gave refuge to Bin Laden for many years. The vacuum of true leadership in the region has forced the US government to soften its policies against rogue nations like Iran. ISIS, al-Qaeda, Hamas, and other terrorist organizations actually make the Islamic Republic of Iran look temperate.

My father told me something just before he passed away that I will never forget. He said Iran is messed up because the shah cursed it for what the Iranians did to him. I laughed when he said that, since I do not believe in curses. But Iran has proved to be one of the worst nations when it comes to a change of governments by revolution. Exchanging the shah for the ayatollah was a curse. We settled for evil just because we were angry at the shah. We, the Iranians, still do not understand democracy. The day that we allow every Iranian to speak his or her mind freely like people do in the West, we will practice democracy. The day we understand that democracy is a good thing and are able to act like the civilized world when confronted with an opposing view, we will be ready for another revolution. Until then, we will remain ceaseless in trying to understand how we can get ourselves out of the misery and darkness of the Islamic Republic of Iran.

There was no way I could have known when I left my home as a high school student to study abroad that I would end up immigrating to the United States while witnessing a catastrophic change of guard in Iran. The Islamic Republic of Iran uprooted my family and thousands of others; it upended a modern society and flung it back several hundred years. The Iranian Revolution is one of the greatest deceptions in the history of humankind. It's our testament to absolute injustice. The oppression in Iran continues to challenge our will, but we, the true children of Cyrus, are untethered. We are relentless in our pursuit to reach the light again. We have lost our way but not our souls.

Made in United States
Orlando, FL
01 February 2022